KT-198-792

20-09-05

⌐is book is to be returned on or
⌐ore the last date stamped below.

⌐als 01702 220447

⌐sex-college.ac.u⌐

30130503933728

OR
09/05

303.483 PUR
HE STL

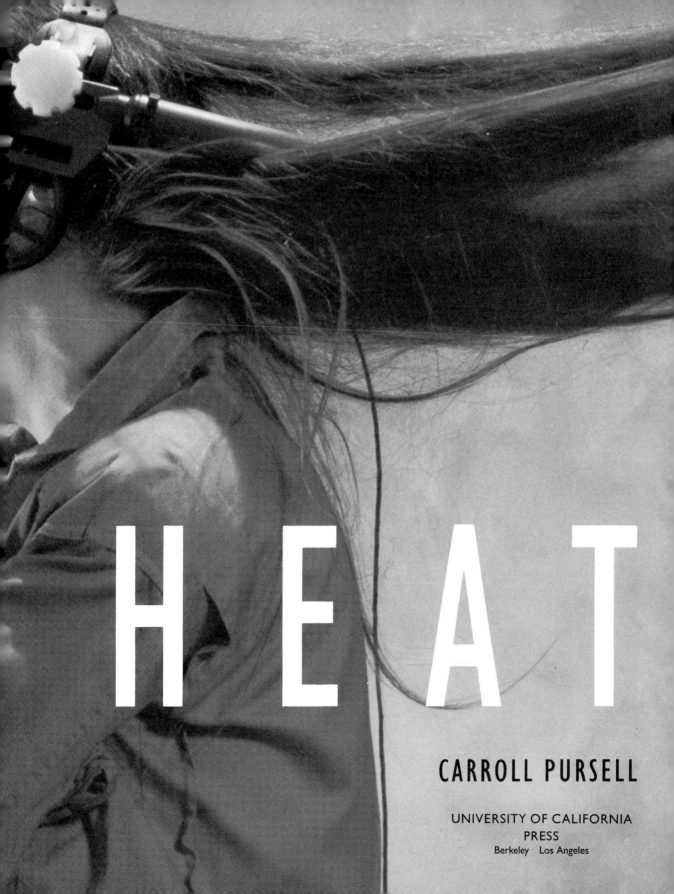

HEAT

CARROLL PURSELL

UNIVERSITY OF CALIFORNIA
PRESS
Berkeley   Los Angeles

PICTURE CREDITS

BBC Books would like to thank the following for providing photographs, and for permission to reproduce copyright material. While every effort has been made to trace and acknowledge all copyright holders, we would like to apologise should there have been any errors or omissions.

Advertising Archives 182, 196, 200; American Museum of Natural History, New York 34; Ann Ronan Picture Library 51 insert left and right, 88, 90, 118, 128, 129, 139, 146, 148, 149, 172, 173, 178, 181, 184, 185; Archiv fur Kunst und Geschichte, Berlin 30, 82; Barnabys Picture Library 41, 71; British Museum 16, 20, 23; The Estate of Mrs William Heath Robinson 92; E.T. Archive 45, 66, 147, 151, 154; Ford Archives 96, 97, 108–9; Hulton-Deutsch 51, 75, 98, 108–9 background, 110, 199; Mander and Mitchenson Theatre Collection 46; The Mansell Collection 125; Punch 24–5, 106, 158, 203, 206, 219; Science Museum 9, 42–3, 64, 147, 68 left, 79, 80, 123, 126, 135 below and right inset; Salisbury Museum 19; Science Photo Library 58, 61, 62, 64, 114, 116, 192, 201; 208, 210, 213, 214, 217; Frank Spooner Pictures 95, 198, 216; The Time Museum 68 right; TRH Pictures 144, 157, 163, 166; Tropix 21; United Airlines 81; The Wellcome Institute for the History of Medicine 191.

University of California Press 1994
Berkeley and Los Angeles, California

Published by arrangement with BBC Enterprises Limited, London, England

© Carroll Pursell, 1994

All rights reserved

Library of Congress Cataloging-in-Publication Data
Pursell, Carroll.
White Heat: People and Technology/Carroll Pursell
p.   cm.
Includes index.
ISBN 0-520-08905-7.

Set in Monotype Old Style by Selwood Systems, Midsomer Norton
Printed and bound by BPC Paulton Books Ltd,
A member of the British Printing Company Ltd
Cover printed by Clays Ltd, St Ives plc

CONTENTS

ACKNOWLEDGEMENTS This book has been a three-way cooperative project, requiring both faith and tolerance in large measures. Henry Singer, Executive Producer of the television programmes for Uden Associates, first involved me in the enterprise and later asked if I might undertake this 'companion volume'. Along with his colleagues at Uden he has been a good friend and active collaborator. Heather Holden-Brown, Commissioning Editor at BBC Books, was willing to take a chance on an author she had yet to meet, and one not able to come up to London regularly for instruction and reassurance. I hope that this book in some measure justifies her faith. My wife and colleague Angela Woollacott, as always, gave me that unqualified support and careful criticism that I have come to depend upon. To all of these I am deeply grateful.

CARROLL PURSELL
CASE WESTERN RESERVE UNIVERSITY
OHIO, USA

PREFACE

This book is intended to be a companion to, not a substitute for, the eight-part television series, 'White Heat'. Like travelling companions, the book and the programmes struck up a conversation before their journeys began. The film-makers were first off the blocks, and had strong, if at first indefinite, notions of where they wanted the series to go. As the interloper, I have accepted those rather broad constraints for the book as well.

The subjects chosen for the eight films left ample room for my own comments and interpretation. On no occasion have I felt the need to contradict my film-making companions. Indeed, one benefit of making this journey with them is that we have each had the opportunity and pleasure of being heard out when, as always, ambiguity needed to be given play and multiple stories clamoured to be heard.

Another advantage arising from this conversation, and one which is entirely congenial to my own taste, is that I was able to make three fundamental decisions before a word was set down.

First, I decided to present my material in something of a collage rather than a linear narrative. This has allowed me to present diverse and sometimes contesting material without facing the necessity of following any one path of development.

Second, I have not felt it necessary in every case to analyse the origins, workings, and consequences of the technologies discussed. Where careful readers might have expected analysis, they will sometimes find irony. I hope that any resulting lack of rigour will be offset by the kind of occasional insight that arises from unresolved juxtapositions.

Third, I have chosen to emphasize representations of technology as often as their reality (though I would insist that the former are just as 'real' as the latter) and to stress technological *meanings* more often than *methods*. It is my belief that to understand technology, how things are made and what they do is often less important than who owns them and how they are used.

With these methodological caveats, this book attempts to be a good companion to the television series. I have repeated, in the appropriate chapters, the main themes of the programmes, set down for more leisurely attention some things about which the viewer might like to know more, and raised both those realities and representations that seem to me related, perhaps even in some important ways.

Chapter 1 The Butcher's Blade examines the relationship between human beings and their technology, and shows how much technology can reveal about the society in which it develops. We see how technology, like language, is fundamental to social organization and is, in fact, one of the enduring symbols of our humanity.

Chapter 2 Out of the Loop investigates the origins of technological innovation, from the stereotype of the eccentric inventor to the corporate teams of 'experts' employed by modern big business and reveals the degree to which change has come from outside the centres of social power.

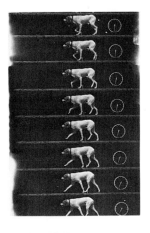

Chapter 3 Step Right Up shows how technology is inextricably involved in our perception of the world around us – particularly that of time and space. The technology with which we organize the world, itself organizes us, just as our culture participates in technology at the same time as being influenced by it.

Chapter 4 Makes No Sense investigates the role of technology in the workplace. The transfer of the artisan's skills to a machine with an 'unskilled' operator caused a massive shift in labour relations. Combined with the management theories of mass production, the worker became another replaceable component in the factory, with identity and creative input severely limited.

Chapter 5 Welcome to the Club addresses the problematic relationship between technology and science. The academic preference for the theoretical over the practical denigrated technological innovation (which tends to evolve in the workplace) in favour of scientific progress (which tends to happen in the laboratory). Hence the inventors of the wheel and the mill are unknown while many scientists have become legendary.

Chapter 6 War in the Age of Intelligent Machines examines the particular pressure exerted on technology to develop ever more lethal weapons. From the stirrup to the 'smart' bomb, each innovation in warfare has been brought about by the desire to kill more people, more efficiently. Hence, human attributes (being 'smart') are attributed to machines, and machine-like attributes (being unfeeling) are imbued into soldiers.

Chapter 7 Dirt and Disorder shows the way in which technology has often developed in tandem with notions of morality in our society. The sewer systems which take away the waste products from the great cities of Europe, for example, are at once a metaphor for the techniques of social control and an actual part of the process. Technology has been instrumental in the human 'conquest' of nature, the implementation of rational structures on the irrational, and as such, is inseparable from our conception of ourselves.

Chapter 8 Information looks to the technology which surrounds the storage and dissemination of information. The advent of the computer has already radically affected the way we work and the way we play, and will continue to do so. However, as information becomes a prime commodity, the potential of information technology as 'information for all' may be wiped out by the disastrous social implications for those unable to access that information.

WHITE HEAT

Chapter one

THE BUTCHER'S BLADE

■ Chorus: *What? Men, whose life is but a day, possess already the hot radiance of fire?*

Prometheus: *They do; and with it they shall master many crafts.*

AESCHYLUS, *Prometheus Bound*[1]

[1] Aeschylus, *Prometheus Bound, The Suppliants, Seven Against Thebes, The Persians* (Harmondsworth: Penguin Books, 1961), p. 28.

A COCA-COLA BOTTLE, a Samurai sword, a Rolls-Royce, and a prehistoric stone tool are linked not only because they are the products of technology, but also because each is a symbol invested with meaning. These objects and products allow us to *do* things; and they also allow us to *say* things – about who we are, what we value, and our place in society. It is a commonplace that technology is an extension of human capabilities, it also projects meaning. Technology is an integral, almost necessary, part of our very claim to being human. By looking for the origins of technology one finds the origins of the human race. The two are inseparable.

Every society must have its creation myths, and science has valiantly tried to provide us with one. As modern people, we in the West are no longer satisfied with tales of Gardens of Eden, turtles floating in the sea, or the delights of other religious explanations. We agree that we have evolved, but at what point, exactly, do we recognize ourselves as distinct from those who were destined not to become us? The physical evidence of our beginnings as human beings has been that which has best resisted many hundreds of thousands of years. We are left with, almost exclusively, bones and stone tools. From these we must infer aspirations, skills, social structures and emotions.

Fortunately tools are rich in meaning. Like any other texts they can be 'read'; careful deconstruction can reveal layers of meanings in their production and use. The making and using of technologies are ritualized and carry significance. Freud may have been right that a cigar is only a good smoke, but he would certainly have been wrong if he had tried to claim that an automobile is merely a form of transport. Many animals survive quite well without technology, and a few even use tools. But if being human means anything, it is difficult to imagine it separate from technology.

The fact that skulls, bones, and stone tools have been found together (should they *all* be referred to as 'human remains'?) has led us to think of our earliest ancestors as *Homo faber*, 'Man the Maker'. Some scholars, however, would press the claim of language, or social organization, as the true indicator of being termed human. But what if, to complicate matters further, all these are equally dependent upon the slow evolution of the human brain? And what if tools are themselves a kind of language, or even a form of social organization?

Like any other scientific 'truth', the answers to these questions are provisional and always evolving. Archaeologists, palaeobiologists, and other scientists who study prehistoric people have been unable to agree on such key parts of the story as whether Neanderthals were our ancestors or an evolutionary dead end. There are many stories, all fascinating, but whichever hypotheses we choose, we can learn a great deal about our own technology, and our relation to it, from them.

As early as the sixteenth century, ancient flints shaped by chipping were recognized as being made by human hands and by the late eighteenth century stone tools made by 'savages' were common enough in the museums of Europe. It appears that it was the American Benjamin Franklin who first used the phrase 'man is a tool-using animal', not a surprising judgement from a man who helped found a nation but styled himself simply as a printer. The same sentiment was later proclaimed by Thomas Carlyle, who wrote in 1841 that 'man is a tool-using animal', adding that 'without tools he is nothing; with them he is all'.[2]

It was only in the early nineteenth century, however, that firm evidence began to accumulate that something like a 'Stone Age' had actually existed. About that time findings from a Danish site seemed conclusive; soon tools were being discovered in other sites, sometimes mixed with the bones of extinct mammals. Then, in 1856, the famous Neanderthal man was discovered in the Neander Valley of Germany.

These developments took place within the context of a widening contact with peoples in Africa, Asia, Australia and the New World. European-Americans for generations before Benjamin Franklin had had good reason to understand the use of stone tools, especially arrowheads, by Native Americans. As the historian Michael Adas notes, with the coming of the Industrial Revolution in the eighteenth century European explorers tended increasingly to judge 'primitive' peoples they encountered in terms of their science and technology. Those using tools most like those preferred by Europeans were thought more 'civilized' than people not doing so. Even more than being judged according to race, he concludes, peoples were given a place along a great continuum according to the perceived evolutionary level of their tools. It became obvious, therefore, that given all the archaeological

[2] Quoted in Gorden W. Hewes, 'A History of Speculation on the Relation Between Tools and Language', in Kathleen R. Gibson and Tim Ingold, *Tools, Language and Cognition in Human Evolution* (Cambridge: Cambridge University Press, 1993), p. 24.

15

and contemporary evidence, there must have been a time when some first peoples appeared, identified by their tools, and that through time some of us evolved into a 'higher' civilization based on superior technologies.

By the nineteenth century it was noticed, however, that some animals, most notably chimpanzees but also some species of birds, fashioned found materials into tools to help crack nuts or get food in other ways. Sea otters off the California coast collect flat stones upon which to crack open the molluscs upon which they feed. It appears that it was not until Jane Goodall's observation of chimps using tools to extract termites from their nests that the real implications of this behaviour began to sink in.

More importantly, speculation about tool use was paralleled by questions about the linguistic abilities of ancient peoples. Those 'discovered' in Africa and the Americas could speak, but what about the Neanderthals? In his *Leviathan*, Thomas Hobbes had insisted that early peoples were sunk in lives without any of the marks of civilization that later peoples enjoyed. Descartes, on the other hand, appeared to believe that speech, like the soul, was a characteristic of people like ourselves and as such, created an unbridgeable gulf between ourselves and any that had gone before. It was a subject that appealed greatly to the broad thinkers of the Enlightenment; Rousseau propounded a theory that allowed for the evolution of both language and tool-making ability.

Without knowing what was possible, it was difficult to detect what was impossible. In 'A History of Speculation on the Relation Between Tools and Language', Gordon W. Hewes recalls the researcher who attempted, in the 1890s, to teach a chimpanzee in London Zoo to count and recognize colours, and reports the contemporary and astonishing news from Africa that chimpanzees had been seen running through the forests carrying torches.[3] Even the new wax-cylinder phonograph was put into use by scientists trying to record the 'vocalizations' of wild primates.

Despite a continuing tradition of speculation on the origins of language and its relationship to the origins and evolution of tool-making, it was not until after the Second World War that our present understanding of the subject began to take shape. The discovery, earlier in the century, of important new fossil hominids like the 'Men' of Heidelberg, Peking, Taung, and Rhodesia and the observing of primates *in situ*, fostered theories on the role of languages and tools.

Main picture and far left: two examples of Acheulian hand axes. Left: a Palaeolithic chopping tool and (above right) a Palaeolithic hand axe.

[3] *Ibid.*, p. 24.

There is now widespread agreement that, about one and a half million years ago, a kind of flaked tool, known as the 'Acheulian hand axe', began to be made by a creature known as *Homo erectus*. These 'axes' (we don't know what they were used for) are handsome, carefully contrived objects fitting into the palm of the hand with remarkable bilateral symmetry. Even more strikingly, they have been discovered at sites on three continents (Asia, Africa and Europe) and in sites more than a million years apart. Until recently technology has always been a profoundly conservative activity. It has been too critical a factor in human survival to invite unnecessary and potentially retrograde variations. The ubiquity and stability of the Acheulian hand axe, however, are stunning.

One possible explanation is that the design of this axe represented a cultural norm, and that successive generations simply learned to make it correctly. A quite different explanation has been that there is really only one way to make a flint axe, hence they all look the same. It has even been suggested that, rather than removing chips of flint (which were then discarded) until the prescribed form was revealed, the chips themselves were the desired product, and the centre from which they had been removed was then thrown away rather like an apple core. In either case, it might be that the axe appeared before language (and the brain size which that implies) and that therefore while *Homo erectus* could reproduce a single design it was not possible, in the absence of language, to develop new designs.

The experimental archaeologist Nicholas Toth has combined the actual making of flint axes with evidence of primate behaviour and hominid remains and come up with one scheme of evolution. He believes that between two and three million years ago somewhere in Africa, our ancestors began to manufacture and use tools made of flaked stone. They had also become right-handed, and this in turn had implications for the development of their (our) brains. *Homo habilis* gave rise, perhaps 1.6 million years ago, to *Homo erectus*, the immediate ancestor of *Homo sapiens*, our own animal group, which appeared about 400 000 years ago. Finally, about 100 000 years ago (or 35 000 years – the claim of Neanderthals to be 'modern' is disputed), 'anatomically modern' humans appeared.

While our ancestors evolved, so too did their technology, although at a strikingly slower pace. The oldest tools, going back about 2.4 million years, were quartz pebbles and rocks that had been shattered deliberately. In sites dating

from 1.8 to 1.9 million years ago these are found in association with bones. Starting from about 1.5 million years ago the new technology of the Acheulian axe is found at sites. These axes were made from stone broken off from rock faces, rather than merely gathered from river beds. They formed the basis for the large double-sided tools usually termed hand axes or cleavers. Although we do not know exactly what these tools were used for, it is important to see them as being a part of a process. First the raw material was acquired, then it was worked upon, then used for some purpose or purposes, and finally discarded. It is this progression that leads archaeologists to see these tools as both shaping and giving evidence of *Homo sapiens* as social creatures.

To help them in understanding the process, Toth and other archaeologists have trained themselves in the art of making stone axes. In fact, their own ancestors can be traced to the nineteenth century when a small, but bothersome, number of forgers produced such tools for the Victorian trade in curiosities. An early photograph of one such English practitioner, Edward 'Flint Jack' Simpson, has survived to document him at his craft. In 1990 Toth and his research team had the good fortune to be able to watch some 'stone-age' people making a traditional stone axe. The Langda people of the New Guinea highlands had traditionally made and traded stone axes and first came into contact with Europeans in 1984.

The Kim-Yal, as Langda people call themselves, live in villages of ten to fifteen huts, containing about 200 people. The making of the stone axes is the monopoly of certain men of the village, who gain great status from this work, as do their sons to whom the mystery of the process is handed down. Lava stones to make the axes, and smaller ones to use as hammers, are taken from a river bed

Above: Edward 'Flint Jack' Simpson, the forger of prehistoric tools, which found a ready market among Victorian collectors of curios, at work.

800 metres below the village. Five to ten blanks are collected and roughed out beside the river, to reduce weight and to reveal any defective pieces. The blanks are then carried back up to the village or to a field hut about 100 metres above the river. Here the artisan rests in the shade, and perhaps cooks some food, as he flakes stone to shape the axe. Often he works sociably in the company of other artisans. They use smaller and smaller hammers to make the axe thinner, narrower and more symmetrical. On returning to the village the artisan takes some last, small and delicate chips from the blade and then grinds it on sandstone. Aesthetic motivation is obvious in the fact that nearly the entire body of the blade, not just its edge, is polished. Red ochre or other pigments are then applied to highlight the depressed parts of the blade.

A villager using one of these blades (which are attached to wooden handles) can fell a tree the size of a telegraph pole in less than ten minutes, and a blade will stay keen for several hours of use before it needs resharpening. When they become blunt to the point of becoming useless, or if they break, they are usually brought back from the fields to the village, because, say the axe makers, they 'feel sorry' for the now useless tool. Good axes are often exchanged as signs of good will or given up as a 'bride price' – compensation to fathers who lose their daughters in marriage. Sadly, years of contact with the West, and particularly missionaries, have led to cultural change, including the gradual dying out of axe-making. By 1992, no young men were apprenticed to learn the craft.

The happy opportunity to be able to watch and record the making of 'stone-age' tools today, however, leads to information that must be used with great care. How much of what was observed might hint at truly ancient practices cannot be known with certainty. Toth suggests that the 'feeling sorry' for the worn and broken axes is probably not of ancient origin, but that the techniques of flaking the blade might well be, especially as they seem to confirm both experimental and archaeological evidence. Doing and thinking are related, but not the same thing. They can, and often do, vary independently of each other.

The hunter-gatherers of stone-age Europe had preferred to use flint nodules that they found lying about on the surface because they had been weathered. With the beginnings of agriculture some 9000 years ago, however, the increased demand for tools led to the extensive mining of flint. At one site studied at

A selection of Palaeolithic flint scrapers discovered in Germany.

Stone tools are still used to this day. This man is using one stone tool to make another which will be used for beating bark into 'cloth' for raincapes in Menyamya in Papua New Guinea.

Rijckholt, in the Netherlands, people mining in neolithic times about 5000 years ago produced flint nodules for a staggering 150 million tools or, assuming that the site was worked for 500 years, some 1500 axe heads per day. Sixty-six vertical shafts have been discovered on only 3000 square metres of the much larger site. The miners built retaining walls to prevent cave-ins as they went down to the chalk beds trough the overburden, and once the flint-bearing chalk was encountered, they used the room-and-pillar construction technique that is still familiar today. The skilled miners themselves used flint tools for digging, sharpening them on the spot when they became blunt. They wore out perhaps up to five or so flint tools in the course of excavating a cubic metre of chalk.

The much-maligned Neanderthals, who flourished 100 000–35 000 years ago, had developed no new tools over that period, but did begin the practice of funerary ritual. The beautiful and apparently gratuitous symmetry of their stone axes show evidence of an aesthetic sense. By contrast, the immediate ancestors of modern humans (often termed Cro-Magnon man), who flourished in the Upper Palaeolithic period (35 000–12 000 years ago), created a virtual explosion of art and technology. Cro-Magnons left evidence of what sometimes appears to be change for the mere sake of change.

The achievements of these people make a long and impressive list. They developed blades which were at least twice as long as they were broad. Thus they provided up to ten times more cutting edge, for the same amount of flint, than was possible with the axe. The blades were attached to handles which produced weapons of exceptional efficiency. The spear thrower, a device for multiplying both the force and accuracy with which a spear could be hurled, also made hunting more efficient. Sometimes these were decorated with animal forms. They made rope and cord, and perhaps nets and snares. They made lamps, using animal oil for fuel and moss for wicks. Some seventy-five per cent of sites that we know about from the period are facing south. This made optimum use of sunlight and conserved fuel. It is a sound form of planning and building that we would do well to remember today. Other innovations of that time included the introduction of a sewing needle with an eye, suggesting tailored clothing, and body adornments like pendants and beads with tiny holes drilled in them.

This appearance of 'jewellery', which has a primarily symbolic purpose, not

*S*ome examples of
Neolithic bowls.

only represents a new level of technological accomplishment, but leads us to believe that symbolic meaning had now become encoded in material objects. This is reinforced by the many clay, stone, ivory, bone and horn statuettes (often 'Venus' figures with an exaggerated female anatomy) and the stunningly beautiful cave paintings and bas-reliefs of southern France and Spain. One figure of a horse, carved into limestone 12 000 years ago, was given several pairs of legs, producing a strong sense of motion. It is hauntingly reminiscent of the experimental photographs taken in the late nineteenth century and of Cubist paintings of the early twentieth. Wind instruments (assumed to be flutes) indicate that music was a part of the life of these first modern people. The anthropologist Randall White, who has called the Upper Palaeolithic age 'A Human Revolution', has concluded that 'it is no coincidence that a burst of symbolic endeavour should accompany one of the greatest periods of technological and social innovation in all of human history.'[4]

As the great ice sheets began to retreat 10 000 years ago, peoples in several places began to experiment with a more settled form of living, most importantly revolving around agriculture and village life. Agricultural technology was developed, as was the use of bowls and pots for collecting, storing and eating foodstuffs. The social critic Lewis Mumford maintained that the 'tendency to identify tools and machines with technology' was merely to 'substitute a part for the whole'. He regretted that one ignored or undervalued the importance of the products of our material culture. Mumford spoke of the containers, or 'static components' of technology: 'hearths, pits, houses, pots, sacks, clothes, traps, bins, byres, baskets, bags, ditches, reservoirs, canals, cities'.[5]

Mumford does not state it explicitly, but his list of 'static components' or 'containers' is profoundly feminine. A pot, when compared with a spear, not only carries suggestions of female rather than male anatomy, it conjures up notions of hearth (another container) and home (yet another) which are profoundly female and domestic in association. From this standpoint, therefore, one might suggest (though Mumford does not) that the origin myths of current science are profoundly masculine in shape and meaning. Other storytellers might tell different stories.

From this point onwards, Mumford sees the development of the 'mega-machine'. Our tendency for the past two centuries to identify technology only

[4] Randall White, 'The Upper Paleolithic: A Human Revolution', p. 49.
[5] Lewis Mumford, 'Technics and the Nature of Man', *Technology and Culture*, 7 (Summer, 1966), 306.

with tools, and then to make these the measure of human progress, is profoundly political since it tends to make natural and perhaps even inevitable, the kind of technological world we now inhabit and continue to elaborate. As Mumford says, 'even the hand was no mere horny work-tool: it stroked a lover's body, held a baby close to the breast, made significant gestures, or expressed in ordered dance and shared ritual some otherwise inexpressible sentiment about life or death, a remembered past or an anxious future. Tool-technics is but a fragment of bio-technics: Man's total equipment for life.'[6] Mumford concludes that, 'at its points of origin, then, technics was related to the whole nature of man, and that nature played a formative part in the development of every aspect of technology; thus, technics at the beginning was broadly life-centered, not work-centered or power-centered.'[7]

The mystery of what could have triggered the 'Human Revolution' described by Randall White and celebrated by Mumford is being attacked on several fronts. Stephen J. Gould and Elisabeth S. Vrba have proposed the term 'exaptations' to describe those characteristics in animals which give them an advantage today, even though they may have evolved originally for a different purpose. Feathers on birds, for example, appear to have evolved perhaps to preserve body heat long before birds were able to fly.[8] Is it possible that technology is just such an 'exaptation', evolved originally to enable people to cut meat and chop wood, but available tens of thousands of years later to solve the growing problem of communication? And might it be that our 'abilities', an *adaptation* of the primate brain, might through *exaptation* enable and explain the evolution of technological 'skills' that continues, ever accelerated, into the present?

The relationship between the size of the neocortex of the brain (the outer surface which is responsible for thought), and the size of social groups has been investigated by the anthropologist Robin Dunbar. She believes that there is a convincing correlation between the size of the neocortex in various primates and the size of the groups within which they live: the smaller the cortex the smaller the group. This suggests to her that keeping track of the other individuals in a group requires the kind of thinking that takes place in the neocortex, and that any need to live in larger groups would give an evolutionary advantage to those individuals or species with larger brains.

[6] *Ibid.*, 307.

[7] *Ibid.*, 310.

[8] Stephen J. Gould and Elisabeth S. Vrba, 'Exaptation – A Missing Term in the Science of Form', *Paleobiology*, 8 (1982), 4–15.

Based on this premise Dunbar calculates that the 'natural' human group would comprise about 150 individuals. She finds a number of human activities that are organized into cohorts of that size. But even this size of group, not to mention cities of many millions and nation states of hundreds of millions of people, make truly 'human' relationships impossible. In groups of primates other than humans, grooming is the primary way of establishing personal relationships, but, as she points out, the time required to groom 149 other people (even if they would permit it) would be prohibitive.

Dunbar suggests that it was language that supplemented grooming (though in the most intimate relationships something like grooming is still popular) and allowed modern humans to gather into larger social relationships. Since even today men talk more often about themselves than do women and women in most situations are put in charge of 'social relationships', Dunbar further suggests that 'language evolved in the context of social bonding between females.'[9]

If Dunbar is correct, her theory might help to explain why technology, along with its cultural complexity, exploded during the Upper Palaeolithic period. Some anthropologists are attempting to expand the notion of a technological system to include more than just the object and its manufacture by looking at it as a fundamentally cultural expression. Thus for Heather Lechtman, 'technological behavior is characterized by the many elements that make up technological activities – for example, by technical modes of operation, attitudes toward materials, some specific organization of labor, ritual observances – elements which are unified nonrandomly in a complex of formal relationships'.[10] She calls 'technological style that which arises from the formal integration of these behavioral events. It is recognizable by virtue of its repetition which allows us to see the underlying similarities in the formal arrangements of the patterns of events.'[11]

What Lechtman and her colleagues want to do is to read the culture of vanished societies in their material culture. Since 'technologies are performances; they are communicative systems, and their styles are the symbols through which communication occurs', they are social expressions which imply both community and meaning. While Lechtman wishes to start with technologies that are culturally encoded and read out of them something about the life and thought of early societies, we can, with both pleasure and profit, reverse the process to learn

[9] Robin Dunbar, 'Why Gossip is Good for You', *New Scientist* (21 November 1992), 31.
[10] Heather Lechtman, 'Style in Technology – Some Early Thoughts', in Heather Lechtman and Robert S. Merrill, eds., *Material Culture: Styles, Organization, and Dynamics of* *Technology* (St. Paul: West Publishing Co., 1977), p. 6.
[11] *Ibid.*, p. 7.

something about ourselves. That is, knowing a good deal about the values and power relationships in our own society (gender systems, for example) we can deconstruct our own technologies to discover the often hidden ways in which their apparent neutrality masks codes of privilege and meaning. The throw-away Coca-Cola bottle tells us a good deal about not only our diet, but our definition of garbage, the geographical reach of Western commercial interests, and the cachet of consumer culture.

It is a complex story that scientists are now constructing out of the contributions of archaeologists, palaeontologists, geologists, geophysicists, animal behaviourists, primatologists, ecologists, anatomists, neurologists, cognitive psychologists, biochemists, molecular biologists, geneticists and social anthropologists (Toth's list, to which should certainly be added linguists and perhaps others). The story hopes to explain how human beings came to have tools and the significance of that development. But there are many ways of explaining this.

The native peoples of California recounted, for example, that fire was given to them by Coyote, a traditional trickster figure always portrayed as a friend and benefactor of the Native Americans. He had used his wit and guile to steal fire from ancient hags who had guarded it jealously. The tale, as detailed by anthropologists, seems to have carried no moral or cautionary message.

For the Greeks Prometheus was not only the benefactor, but, by some accounts, also the creator of humankind. He stole fire from Olympus to give it to mankind. Born of the Earth and fathered by a god, Prometheus was not only a Titan, but the first endowed with rational and moral qualities. Foreseeing that cunning was soon to replace brute strength in the rule of the universe, he sided with Zeus and became a patron of humanity. In his play, *Prometheus Bound,*[12] Aeschylus wrote that, before Prometheus, people had 'eyes, but sight was meaningless; Heard sounds, but could not listen; all their length of life they passed like shapes in dreams, confused and purposeless'. Prometheus reveals that 'their every act was without knowledge, till I came', and the list of technologies, of skills and mysteries that he gave humanity was comprehensive.

'I taught them,' he tells the Greek Chorus, 'to determine when stars rise or set ... Number, the primary science, I invented for them, and how to set down words in writing.' He showed them how to harness animals to pull heavy loads,

'The most common piece of disposable technology!'

[12] Aeschylus, *Prometheus Bound, The Suppliants, Seven Against Thebes, The Persians* (Harmondsworth: Penguin Books, 1961).

gave them drugs and the art of medicine, and told how to interpret dreams. 'No one before me discovered the sailor's waggon – flax-winged craft that roam the seas,' and 'next the treasures of the earth, the bronze, iron, silver, gold hidden deep down . . .'. Summing up, 'All human skill and science was Prometheus' gift.'

Angry at this bounty for an imperfect humanity, Zeus forbade Prometheus to give it the final gift of fire as well. When the latter disobeyed and, like Coyote, stole fire from the gods, he was condemned to be chained to a rock and have his liver pecked out each day by a great bird. The Chorus, which seems generally sympathetic to the plight of Prometheus, is aghast at the gift of fire. Prometheus tells them with pride that 'fire has proved for men a teacher in every art, their grand resource'. But the chorus takes a rather different view crying: 'What? Men, whose life is but a day, possess already the hot radiance of fire?'

It is significant that, in the opinion of the Chorus, it was the temporal nature of humanity that made it unfit to be trusted with fire. The million years of stability in the design of flint axes has been replaced, in modern times, by a constant search for novelty and 'improvement'. The Chorus would not have been surprised that a monumental statue of Prometheus was erected by the Soviets in front of the Chernobyl nuclear power plant; only at the hubris that their warning was ignored. The need we now have to keep that crippled and radioactive reactor isolated for up to 100 000 years violates that very principle of which the Promethean chorus warned. The tombs of the Egyptian Pharaohs were breached within 5000–10 000 years; the cracks in the concrete sarcophagus of Chernobyl are already so wide that birds fly in and out.

When Mary Shelley subtitled her novel, *Frankenstein*, 'The Modern Prometheus', she gave the reader a clear indication that it was Victor Frankenstein's relationship with his technology that lay at the heart of the story. The monster (that it was never given a name by its 'father' is a powerful refusal of responsibility) was a cunning imitation of life, a technology at once powerful, terrible and efficient. It was, moreover, a technology intimately connected in meaning and purpose with its creator. It is entirely proper that so many people apply the inventor's name to his invention. The monster is, quite simply, the active agent of Victor Frankenstein's own worst self, the self of forbidden emotions assigned to perform crimes of passion. It is for this reason that Frankenstein refuses ever to destroy

Piero di Cosimo's sixteenth-century painting of the story of Prometheus.

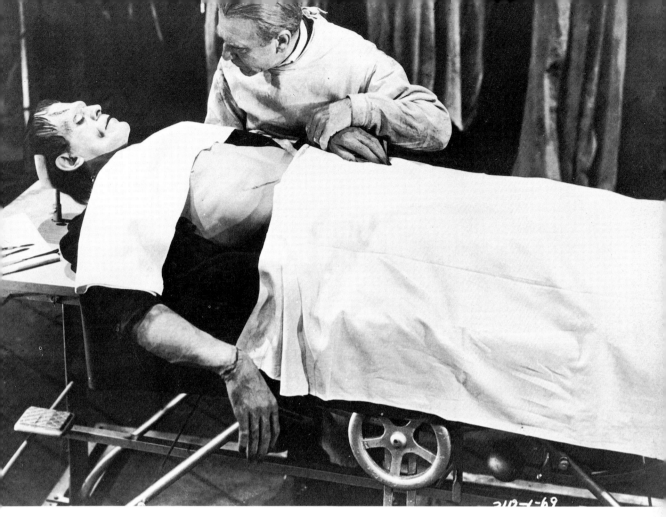

or control his creation; his technology does his work. His protests of horror are hypocritical posturing.

The agony of Hephaestus in his relationship with his craft of smith seems more genuine. The god of fire and son of Zeus, he was chosen to bind Prometheus to the rock. When Strength and Violence drag the unhappy Prometheus to his place of imprisonment, Hephaestus cries out: 'I hate my craft, I hate the skill of my own hands.' Taking a modern and rather professional view of the matter, Strength asks: 'Why do you hate it? Take the simple view: your craft is not to blame for what must be inflicted now.'

The attitude towards technology in the Greek myths is particularly revealing

Mary Shelley's modern Prometheus — Frankenstein and his monster as millions of film audiences remember them.

in helping us think about this subject in the late twentieth century. In the legend Hephaestus was lame. The accounts of how he became so are varied, but the meaning is more certain. As a cripple, he was unfit to be either warrior or farmer. Perhaps he took up a craft as a result, suggesting a less manly calling? Though handicapped, he appears to have been attractive to beautiful women, marrying at last the faithless Aphrodite. This marriage of beauty with the useful arts reminds us that much of the earliest extant metalwork is in the museums of the world, where its utilitarian and aesthetic characteristics combine to delight both the eye and mind.

It is in this tradition that the word 'art' has a continuing and ambiguous meaning. The term technology, as we use it, dates only from the early nineteenth century. Before that time what we now mean by that word would have been called the arts or, more specifically, the useful arts. The words art, artisan, and artificial all come from the Latin word *ars*, and reinforce the notion that beauty and utility have traditionally been inextricably linked. The jazz musician Duke Ellington is believed to have said that if any music sounds good, it is good. The beauty of utility goes back at least as far as the flint axe and is as contemporary as the supersonic Concorde.

The finding of beauty and, more broadly, meaning in technology, appears to be basic to both the technology and our humanity. On one level this has profound political implications. It was Aristotle who suggested that every technology had three characteristics: design (or shape, extension), substance (material), and intention, and that from a knowledge of any of these one could make intelligent guesses about the others. If one's intention, for example, was to carry water, this would suggest something about the proper shape of the object and the substance from which it should be made. In the seventeenth century, those who sought to act as midwife to the birth of modern science were adamant about discarding Aristotle's formula, since intention suggested some plan in the mind of God which was, by definition, beyond the powers of experiment and the reason of researchers. Thus the question of *why* a clam is shaped as it is could be labelled unscientific – a riddle for the clergy or the poet perhaps, but not for the scientist.

In whichever way such a rejection aided the development of science, it made little sense in terms of technology. Indeed, intention was at the very heart of technology. To try to invent something without any idea of what it was supposed to do stretched credulity beyond limit. The purpose might be what archaeologists who deal with a specific period call *tectonic* (strictly utilitarian), *socio-technic* (used to convey social messages), or *ideo-technic* (used to signify religious or ideological messages) – or some combination of the three. James Deetz has suggested that our material culture (whether stone tool or family car) is 'that sector of our physical environment that we modify through culturally determined behavior'.[13] If this is accepted all technology has meaning in the cultural sense, and is not limited to utility. The utility of a tool is never simply in the production of *goods*; the tool also produces *meaning*.

It is important to remember, however, that although designers may have one or more intention in mind, they cannot control the meanings that others place upon their inventions. Perhaps it is the old Platonic prejudice favouring 'knowing' over 'doing' that encourages our society to value the design of technology over its production, and its production over consumption, with maintenance hardly considered at all. But the intention of an inventor that a certain machine shall produce pins neither anticipates nor controls the meanings that workers may put upon that machine – marks of skill and masculinity, for example, or alienation and feminization. The inventors of such weapons as the submarine, the machine gun and the atomic bomb have all insisted that the 'meaning' of their terrible contributions is that war would now be impossible, so frightful would be the carnage. One premise of the popular 1984 film, *The Gods Must Be Crazy*, was that while a Coke bottle might be encoded with certain meanings by its maker, other meanings could be constructed by those who discarded it and those who found it.

The story of evolutionary progress itself has 'meaning'. Sir Peter Medawar has said he believes that the evolutions of people and their tools have not only paralleled each other, but interacted. Asserting that 'all instruments are functionally parts of ourselves', he has even claimed that the 'proxy evolution of human beings through exosomatic instruments has contributed more to our biological success than the conventional evolution of our own (or "endosomatic") organs'. Thus as we elaborate our technology we shape ourselves. Nor is this the end; he looks forward now to a period 'in which the whole human ambience, the human house, is of our own making and becomes as we intend it should be, a

[13] James Deetz, *In Small Things Forgotten: The Archaeology of Early American Life* (Garden City: Anchor Books, 1977), p. 24.

33

product of human thought...'[14] He was referring to the word 'ecology', taken from the Greek *oikos* for house, and he recommended 'forethought' to help preserve it. The confidence he expressed in humanity's ability to take over complete control of the evolution of all life thoughtfully is stunningly optimistic. Whether or not the meaning he drew from the evolutionary story warrants such faith can be disputed, but only with reference to some other meaning or some other story.

In the spring of 1993, the American Museum of Natural History in New York City unveiled its new Hall of Human Biology and Evolution. The word evolution

A diorama of the famous 'Lucy', an early hominid discovered in the 1970s.

[14] Peter Medawar, 'What's human about Man is his technology', *Smithsonian*, 4 (May, 1973), 22, 28.

appears in the very name of the hall, but *The New York Times* reported sardonically that, 'while evolution is discretely threaded through the entire exhibit, no family trees or other evolutionary diagrams are displayed'. The museum's palaeo-anthropologist explained that, 'scientific thinking about evolutionary pathways, particularly those leading to modern man, is changing so rapidly that they cannot be represented too specifically in an exhibition intended to be permanent'.[15]

Early in the century the bully figure of Teddy Roosevelt, former president and African big game hunter, stood at the entrance to the museum which featured such life-like exhibits as a family of stuffed gorillas. It has not escaped the notice of recent scholars that the patriarchal family portrayed in the scene nicely reflected a social belief that the nuclear family was the 'natural' organization of human kinship groups. The father gorilla loomed menacingly forward, as though to protect his family; mother gorilla hung back and adopted a protective gesture towards her children. It was, indeed, a very bourgeois domestic scene; one suspects that the scientists of the period wanted very much to find in nature that which they considered natural in human society. Indeed the further notion that 'savage' peoples from Australian Aborigines to Native Americans belonged with the stuffed gorillas in a 'natural history' museum rather than an 'historical' museum, seems to raise profoundly political issues.

One of the new dioramas in New York strikes a startlingly contemporary note. Two early hominids, *Australopithecus afarensis*, are shown walking across a desolate landscape, leaving behind the footprints discovered by Mary Leakey in Tanzania. One of the figures is that of the famous 'Lucy', discovered in Ethiopia in the 1970s. The other figure is a male, and he walks with his arm affectionately around Lucy's shoulders.[16] The representation echoes the recent suggestions of primatologists that, in at least some contemporary species, females prefer to mate not with the largest and strongest males, but with those which are the kindest to them.

The Museum of Natural History could not entirely resist the urge to add cultural significance to the new exhibit. As one enters the hall one discovers a display case 'in which the skeleton of a female gorilla extends her finger toward the outstretched finger of a skeletal woman. "We were thinking of the Sistine Chapel and Michelangelo's *Creation of Adam*,"' explained the curator.[17]

[15] *The New York Times*, 23 April 1993.
[16] *Science*, 260 (23 April 1993), p. 495.
[17] *Ibid.*

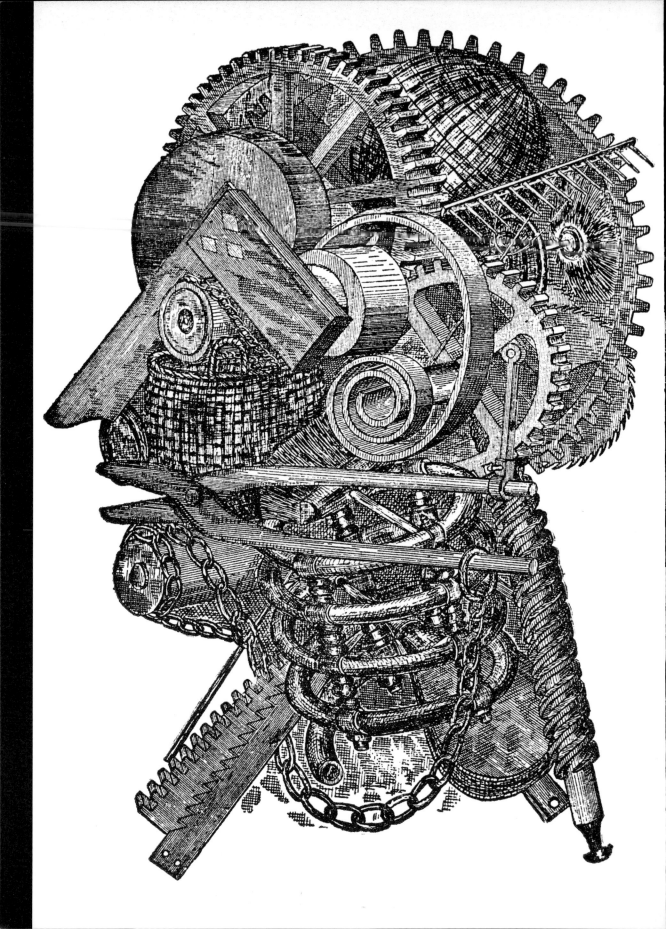

Chapter two

OUT
OF THE
LOOP

■ *Inventing is a lot of
fun, if you don't have to make
a living at it.*

JACOB RABINOW, *Inventor*[1]

[1] Quoted in Edmund L. Andrews, 'The Illogical Process of Invention', *New York Times*, 5 May 1990.

GYRO GEARLOOSE, WALT DISNEY'S cartoon inventor, is popular in Brazil, where he is known as 'Professor' Gearloose. The honorific is undeserved but significant. For Brazilians, since he is an inventor, and inventions are the result of scientific research, and scientific research is done in universities, Gyro obviously is a professor. In the American original, however, Gearloose is an 'independent' inventor, so impractical that he must tie his hat on his head or lose it; while his inventions always do *something*, they never do exactly what he intends. In contrast to Walt Disney's evil scientist Dr Kronos, who works for an illegal power (the criminal Mr Big), Gearloose often works for legitimate power, the fabulously wealthy capitalist, 'Uncle' Scrooge McDuck.

The American view of Scrooge and the Brazilian perception of Gearloose tell us a great deal about popular beliefs about inventors. First, inventions don't emerge out of the blue, they are created by someone. Second, inventors need support from somewhere. It is (and always has been) an expensive and complicated process to move from an idea to a product. Third, no object has only one use, and even the inventor is not always the best person to predict the many possible ways in which an invention may be used. Surprises are always to be expected. Fourth, inventors in our own time have acquired a reputation for, at the very least, eccentricity and, at the extreme, a kind of madness. Finally, the perception of the origin of inventions has shifted in this century from being the work of the individual genius to that of the trained expert, usually working in a scientific laboratory which is a part of some larger organization.

Gyro Gearloose's eccentricity and lack of institutional attachment highlight one fundamental truth: almost by definition, new products, processes and attitudes must come from outside the status quo. Marginality is no bad quality in an inventor but one can be on the outside in a number of ways – outside the industry or firm, the academy or court, the standards of bourgeois respectability. One can be ignorant, perhaps, of accepted practice; be of the wrong sex, race, religion, or belong to the wrong class.

There are at least three myths that colour our views on the source of invention. The most difficult to refute, because it is based on a semi-religious faith in the inevitability of progress, is the belief that technology develops out of its own inevitable and irresistible logic. This view is neatly expressed in the phrase 'if it can be done, it will be done'. The notion is that a kind of invisible hand guides technology ever onward and upward, using individuals and organizations as vessels for its purposes but guided by a sort of divine plan for bringing the greatest good to the greatest number. Technological improvement has been the best evidence for progress so far in this otherwise disappointing world, where virtue and wisdom seem no further ahead than they were two millennia ago.

Putting the mystical belief in technology to one side however, one can best test the proposition by looking at technologies which, while possible, are still not widely in use. Architectural design of buildings that makes best use of the sun's light, for example, goes back at least as far as the ancient Greeks, but even now seems exotic and somehow futuristic. Active solar devices, like those for heating water, were commercially available in the United States in the late nineteenth century and widely used in Southern California early in this century. They too, however, are considered untested and possibly practical only sometime in the future. Solar-voltaics, the direct conversion of sunlight into electricity, has some limited use today, but receives only a small fraction of the research and development attention that is lavished on such truly speculative power sources as laser fusion. There are no doubt a number of reasons for such a situation, but the fact remains that while all three solar technologies 'can be done', largely they are not.

A second myth, perhaps related to the first, is that invention is driven by market forces. Again, a common saying sums it up: 'necessity is the mother of invention'. The father of invention has apparently not stepped forward to take credit for his part in the process. One recent commentator has charged that the 'reality, more often than not, is almost exactly the reverse: invention is the mother of necessity'.[2] Not only were some inventions not 'needed', they were absolutely rejected by society when they first appeared. Often this rejection comes from the manufacturers, who see no reason to introduce 'better' ways of doing whatever their regular products do already. At other times, manufacturers market the inventions but nobody buys them. The telephone with a small television screen, allowing callers to see each other, was a resounding flop when it was introduced some years ago.

[2] Ibid.

The parking meter demonstrates the complexity of the idea of 'need'. The city of San Francisco is home to 464 100 vehicles – this means that there are 10 313 per square mile of the city. The city also has 21 000 parking meters. Why are they there? One can imagine that, originally, some inventor 'needed' to make an invention, because that is the way they make a living. The devices themselves, clever and straightforward combinations of clock and coin-operated vending machines, are manufactured by firms that 'need' products to sell.

The city of San Francisco 'needs' the revenue produced, although the US $10 891 000 raised in 1991–2 needs to be compared to the US $5000 000–6000 000 spent thus far to repair vandalized machines and in lost revenue. Local merchants 'need' the meters to keep some motorists, perhaps commuters, from taking up the space in front of their shops for the entire day, and shoppers 'need' them so that after several futile circles of the block, they may eventually find a place to park their cars.[3]

Many of these 'needs' arise from the fact that people drive cars rather than walk or use public transport; and all these needs could be met in some other way. Many modern 'needs' are themselves inventions, the product of an economy that stimulates consumption so that it can make and market things for a profit. To dignify these with the term 'needs' is simply to obscure rather than explain where inventions come from. The word 'need' carries vague implications of inevitability, and its 'filling' by business seems tinged somehow with a spurious benevolence.

'Inventiveness', the historian Brooke Hindle writes, 'was, of course, responsive to needs, but it often looked for the need after a possible invention had arisen in the mind.' With organic evolution, he concluded, 'positive mutations are selected for perpetuation; just as inventive ideas may be selected for development when they prove applicable to social and economic needs – or even when such needs can be aroused'.[4]

The third presumed source of invention is the classic inventor, a 'genius' who, like the Romantic artist, draws on springs of creativity both noble and mysterious. This idea is firmly entrenched in our popular culture and written into law through the concept of the 'flash of genius' that legally defines the moment of inspired design. Like the artist too, inventors have often been seen as misunderstood dreamers, half-mad perhaps, thriving in isolated workshops, and rewarded only long after their deaths.

[3] *San Francisco Chronicle*, 26 May 1993.
[4] Brooke Hindle, *Emulation and Invention* (New York: New York University Press, 1981), p. 128.

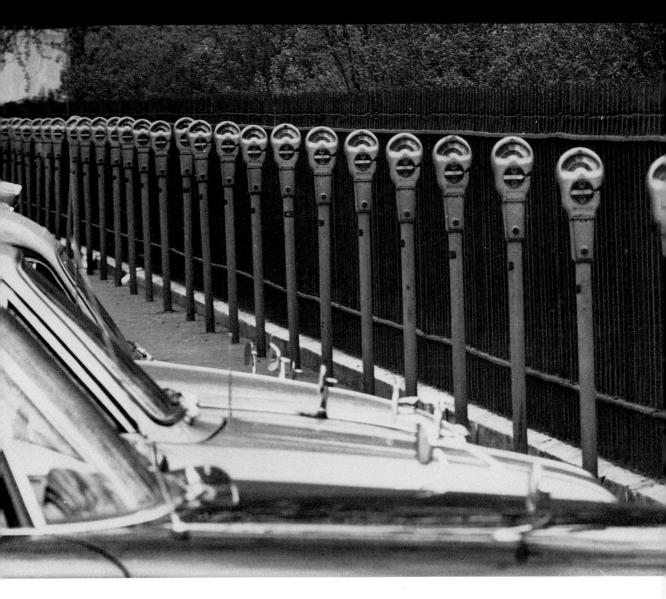

The inventor as a characteristic social type appeared only in the eighteenth century. For millennia technological change had been slow and anonymous: the truly great inventions such as fire, the wheel and the cornmill have no names, or even dates, ascribed to them. In part this was because while science had always been associated with the court and church, practised by learned scholars often known to history, new technologies arose from humble workers and artisans, often illiterate and socially anonymous.

Above: parking meters in London — an invention born out of necessity?

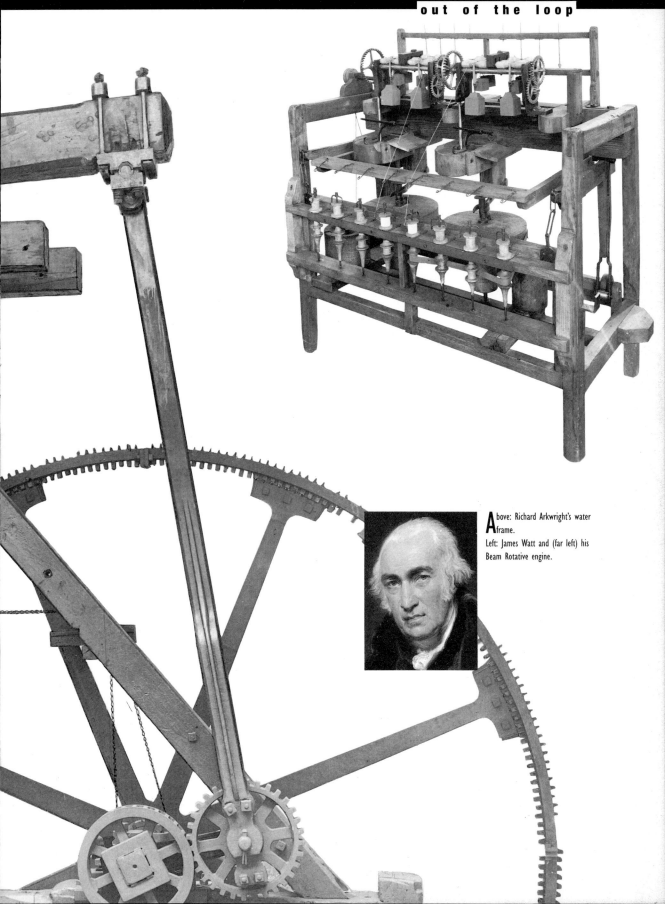

Above: Richard Arkwright's water frame.
Left: James Watt and (far left) his Beam Rotative engine.

It is with the Industrial Revolution that such names as Newcomen and Watt, Arkwright and Cort, leap from the accounts of industrial progress, as people who through their individual genius and perseverance created tools, machines, and processes which had not existed before. The nineteenth century was the great age of heroes, and romantic notions of genius were grafted onto an older, Renaissance, celebration of the individual.

Scientific study of genius flourished, allowing one enthusiast to claim, in 1896, that, 'looking at this campaign of progress from an anthropological and geographic standpoint, it is interesting to note who are its agents and what its scenes of action. It will be found that almost entirely the field [of invention] lies in a little belt of the civilized world between the 30th and 50th parallels of latitude of the western hemisphere and between the 40th and 60th parallels of the western part of the eastern hemisphere, and the work of a relatively small number of the Caucasian race under the benign influences of a Christian civilization.'[5] Of the idols of Anglo-American Victorian culture, only capitalism was unacknowledged.

Rather than being seen as paragons of Victorian virtue and respectability, inventors were often viewed as misfits, ill-suited to polite society. The historian Elting Morison made an informal study of thirty or so nineteenth-century inventors. He found that 'a surprising number turned out to be people with little formal education, who drank a good deal, who were careless with money, and who had trouble with wives or other women'. The out-of-control masculinity in this description is palpable. If, indeed, inventors exhibited these characteristics more commonly than other men of their time (which may or may not be true), then perhaps Morison is correct in suggesting that we can 'look upon invention as a hostile act – a dislocation of existing schemes, a way of disturbing the comfortable bourgeois routines and calculations, a means of discharging the restlessness with arrangements and standards that arbitrarily limit'.[6] If this sounds rather bohemian now we should remember that the words artist and artisan have a common root, and so, it was believed, did genius.

In the Spring of 1993 newspapers reported that 'a British inventor has stunned military and scientific experts by creating a plastic tough enough to withstand heat from nuclear explosions'. Perhaps it was the physical properties of this 'variety of 21 polymers, copolymers, ceramic and additives' that 'stunned'

[5] Quotation from Edward Byrn in Robert Friedel, 'Perspiration in Perspective: Changing Perceptions of Genius and Expertise in American Invention', *Inventive Minds: Creativity in Technology*, ed. Robert J. Weber and David N. Perkins (New York: Oxford University Press, 1992), p. 16.

[6] Elting E. Morison, *Men, Machines, and Modern Times* (Cambridge: MIT Press, 1966), p. 9.

the experts, but just as surely their surprise sprang in part from the fact that the inventor, Maurice Ward, was said to be a businessman and 'a former hairdresser with no university training'.[7] One thinks of that other hairdresser, Richard Arkwright, whose eighteenth-century water frame was a key invention in the shift from hand to power spinning in the transformation of the textile industry. Like those who find it difficult to believe that Shakespeare could really have written his plays, doubters often are 'stunned' to find new ideas coming from inappropriate sources; from people too far outside the loop.

These people were considered unlikely to be inventors because of a variety of reasons. In the early years of the Industrial Revolution, a remarkable group of people met in the Birmingham Lunar Society. They were individuals active in commerce, finance, manufacturing, science, and the 'useful arts'. A surprising proportion of them were religious dissenters: people kept, by law, from the full range of civic participation in British society. It seems not unlikely that some of that thwarted drive was channelled into economic and technological innovation – innovation which did much to destroy the very privileges which they were denied.

Engineers, like inventors, were designers of the emerging machine society, and they too came to prominence as people helping to construct a new world in the eighteenth century. The first generation or two made up what historian R.A. Buchanan calls 'a motley crew'. Most of them, he points out, 'were artisans, practical craftsmen from humble homes and lacking in any formal education, although many of them had served apprenticeships as millwrights, mechanics, instrument makers, or stonemasons'.[8]

We are informed by Samuel Smiles that the great James Brindley, a member of the first generation of civil engineers, 'could scarcely read, and he was thus cut off, to his own great loss, from familiar intercourse with a large class of cultivated minds, living and dead; for he could not share in the conversation of educated men, nor enrich his mind by reading the stores of experience found treasured up in books. Neither could he write, except with difficulty and inaccuracy ...'[9]

It was perhaps for this reason that, according to his brother-in-law, 'when any extraordinary difficulty occurred to Mr Brindley in the execution of his works, having little or no assistance from books or the labours of other men, his resources lay within himself. In order, therefore, to be quiet and uninterrupted whilst he

[7] (Cleveland) Plain Dealer, 2 May 1993.

[8] R.A. Buchanan, 'Gentlemen Engineers: The Making of a Profession', Victorian Studies, 26 (Summer, 1983), 410–11.

[9] Samuel Smiles, Selections from Lives of the Engineers, with an account of their principal works, ed. Thomas Parke Hughes (Cambridge: MIT Press, 1966), p. 166.

was in search of the necessary expedients, he generally retired to his bed; and he was known to be there one, two, or three days, till he had attained the object in view. He would then get up and execute his design, without any drawing or model. Indeed, it was never his custom to make either, unless he was obliged to do it to satisfy his employers.'[10]

These stories about Brindley, albeit filtered through the imagination of the nineteenth century's pre-eminent celebrant of technical genius, are revealing in several ways. Like many inventors, Brindley was a person of humble origins and limited formal education, more comfortable communing with things than with people, and at his best when withdrawn from social interaction and distraction.

A scene from Capek's play *R.U.R.* which concerned the rise and fall of robots.

[10] Quoted in Smiles, p. 168.

Thomas Hughes, in sketching the characteristics of independent inventors at the turn of the twentieth century, observes that 'aware of the unorthodoxy of their ideas, inventors and [avant-garde] artists intensified their feelings of being outsiders by their physical withdrawal. Working in their retreats, intellectual and physical, they created a new way, even a new world, to displace the existing one.'[11]

Literature is dotted with such stories. In the brothers Capek's play *R.U.R.*, the invention, development, and manufacture of robots take place on an unidentified island far from Europe and the markets for their machines. In Franz Kafka's story *The Penal Colony*, the terrible and complicated machine for bringing enlightenment and death to offenders is designed, constructed, and used in a typically Kafkaesque landscape which is nowhere, but could be anywhere. In the film *Things to Come*, based on the H.G. Wells novel, scientists and engineers withdraw from England to an isolated island after a terrible world war, there to perfect a great air armada capable of recapturing the country from the barbarian hordes which roam its blighted landscape.

Paradoxically, though perhaps not surprisingly, the early engineers longed for the very trappings of respectability and institutions for conviviality which they did not inherit by birth. John Smeaton, atypical in that he came from a middle-class background, was the first to style himself a civil engineer, and was also the first to take steps toward forming, in Britain, the Society of Civil Engineers, in 1771. It has been noted that the British gentlemen's club is specifically designed to segregate its members behind protective walls of class and gender privilege, and so it was with the organizations of the engineers.

The three ancient professions of the law, medicine, and the cloth, were joined as the Industrial Revolution wore on, by a host of others, from librarian, to nurse, to teacher. The new engineering profession, however, was one of the first and largest. Like the mining engineer in Emile Zola's novel *Germinal*, however, the position was often purchased at the cost of becoming de-classed. Born to the working class, never quite accepted by their betters, the engineers often adopted conservative political and economic attitudes and, in Britain at least, sometimes abandoned the profession altogether as soon as their accumulated earnings allowed them to become a part of the rural gentry.

Apart from the desire for isolation, the other striking element in the Brindley

[11] Thomas P. Hughes, *American Genesis: A Century of Invention and Technological Enthusiasm, 1870–1970* (New York: Viking, 1989), p. 24.

story is his ability to visualize his technical problems and their solutions, to the extent, even, that he had no need to make drawings or models. Again, the classic stories of inventors often emphasize this same element. The Rumanian-American inventor Nicola Tesla, who is best remembered for developing the technology for alternating current (AC) electricity, claimed that he could design, test, alter and perfect a new device entirely in his imagination, so that the resulting machine, when built, would operate perfectly. Robert Fulton, 'father' of the steamboat, was an artist by training, and Samuel F.B. Morse, inventor of the electric telegraph, was a professor of art in New York City.

Whether these inventors drew more on the right hemisphere of the brain (seat of visual, auditory and tactile inputs) than from the left (which handles speech and calculation), Brooke Hindle points out that they drew upon their artistic talents and training to enable them to choose among numerous design solutions. Further, it was a distinct advantage to be able to picture spatially the way in which design components might be put together in systems and how they could be connected. The 'contriving mind', is the term Hindle uses to characterize this configuration of abilities.

Eugene Ferguson, a mechanical engineer turned historian, has studied a similar talent among the great engineers of the past. 'Until the 1960s', he maintains, 'a student in an American engineering school was expected by his teachers to use his mind's eye to examine things that engineers had designed – to look at them, listen to them, walk around them, and thus develop an intuitive "feel" for the way the material world works and sometimes doesn't work.' The ability to 'see' with the 'mind's eye' is being lost, he fears, with the result that the art of design (perhaps in invention, as well as engineering) is losing out to a mindless dependence on mathematics and computer models. 'Nearly all engineering failures', he warns, 'result from faulty judgements rather than faulty calculations.'[12]

How the process of invention proceeded, that is, how the flash of genius actually wound up on the shelf, has been the subject of much speculation. The economist and pioneer historian of technology, Abbott Payson Usher, postulated that four steps were involved:

1. *Perception of a problem*, in which 'an incomplete or unsatisfactory pattern' in need of resolution is recognized

[12] Eugene S. Ferguson, 'How Engineers Lose Touch', *American Heritage Invention and Technology*, 8 (Winter, 1993), 16, 20.

2. *Setting the stage*, in which 'all data essential to a solution' is found either through 'pure chance' or 'the mediated contingency of a systematic effort to find a solution by trial and error'

3. *Act of insight*, 'by which the essential solution of the problem is found'

4. *Critical revision*, in which a solution is fully explored and revised and even open to new acts of insight.[13]

Usher's rather neat formula is not the only one that has been proposed. Recently the psychologist Michael E. Gorman and the historian of technology W. Bernard Carlson have suggested that inventors create 'mental models' that incorporate 'his or her assumption about how a device might eventually work'. This mental model is then embodied in what they call a 'mechanical representation'. Finally, they suggest that 'the strategies and tactics that an inventor uses to bring together mental models and mechanical representations are *heuristics*', that is, a method of learning through discovery.

In an ingenious exercise, Gorman and Carlson test their formula against the ways in which Alexander Graham Bell and Thomas Edison attacked the problem of the telephone. The reality of their environment was that Bell, in seeking to improve telegraph transmission, hit upon a different phenomenon: the possibility of voice transmission. The inventor Elisha Gray had, in fact, done the same thing, but being a professional inventor he had simply made a note of it and gone on with his original problem. Being an amateur inventor – he made a living as a teacher of the deaf – Bell was free to tackle another problem and invent the telephone. With his patents, Bell created a monopoly which the American telegraph giant Western Union proposed to evade by hiring Edison to invent an alternative technology.

The study of different ways in which Bell and Edison went about their tasks is instructive. According to Gorman and Carlson, Bell tended to manipulate his mental model before finally, with help from his assistant Watson, embodying it in a mechanical representation. Edison, on the other hand, tended to focus on a clear and relatively constant mental model while manipulating his mechanical representation until he got it right. As a result, Bell created the telephone where none had existed before, while Edison invented a better one.

[13] Quoted from David A. Hounshell, 'Invention in the Industrial Research Laboratory: Individual Act or Collective Process?', *Inventive Minds: Creativity in Technology*, ed. Robert J. Weber and David N. Perkins (New York: Oxford University Press, 1992), p. 285.

By the early 1900s, as Robert Friedel has shown, the popular image of the independent genius-inventor had been largely replaced by a new social type, the 'expert'. With the steady elaboration of professions, an increasing access to higher education, and soaring prestige for science, the genius was displaced by the well-trained expert. Information was valued over insight and the rational over the intuitive. The social goals of rationalization and efficiency changed the way in which natural resources were exploited (conservation), labour was marshalled (scientific management), and even the way in which technological change was accomplished.

The process can be seen clearly in the transformation of the electrical industry in the United States during the last years of the nineteenth century. As independent inventors such as Thomas Edison attempted to develop, manufacture, and market their new devices, they came to need the talents of business management and salesmanship, as well as large amounts of capital investment. At the same time, competing inventions made it increasingly difficult to put together the best technical systems and to integrate systems without patent pools or some other form of consolidation.

In this climate, inventors bought each other out, and when they went to finance capitalists, like J.P. Morgan, the latter provided money only on condition that, as investor, they had a significant say in the resulting enterprises. The firm of Thomson-Houston, for example, was the result of the merged interests of those two pioneer electrical inventors. Using Morgan money this firm bought out Edison and changed its name to Edison General Electric, although the world's most famous, and arguably successful, inventor lost control of his inventions in the process. The new giant firm also controlled the patents of Frank Sprague, the 'father' of American tram technology and Charles Brush, who developed the nation's first successful arc-lighting system.

General Electric, heavy with patents from some of America's most ingenious electrical inventors, had also cut them out of the circle and thereby isolated itself from the very wellsprings of its technological advantage. Because companies wanted to ensure that funds were spent on production and sales, not simply more 'progress', inventors found their freedom severely limited. Most had no desire to become corporate bureaucrats in any case, and went on to invent in other fields.

■ *The patent system . . .
added the fuel of interest to the
fire of genius in the discovery
and production of new and
useful things.*

ABRAHAM LINCOLN, *1859*[14]

Right: Alexander Graham Bell and
(far right) Thomas Edison.

This large corporation then, was left with a market share based on inventions which were likely some day to be replaced – but by what, and invented by whom? The initial strategy was to remain alert to the light bulbs going off over the heads of inventors all over the world, with the intention of buying the resulting patents or at least the American rights to the new devices. It was by definition a chancy and unpredictable business.

In 1900 General Electric established its famous research laboratory in Schenectady, New York. It was to be, in a sense, an organized, rationalized, predictable analogue to the creative geniuses who had made the original invention upon which the firm's product line was based. The laboratory, in the words of one historian, reflected and reinforced the 'modern notion of technical change owing more to institutions and less to individuals, of invention as being the province of corporations and not of wizards, of human minds and knowledge making a difference in the way people live and work and die not through creative brilliance but through organization and control.'[15]

The General Electric Research Laboratory gained an enormous reputation as an idea factory, highlighted in 1932 by the award of the Nobel Prize to one of its star researchers, Irving Langmuir. Although perhaps not the first such industrial laboratory (it depends on how the term is defined), GE's was soon joined by a host of others, on both sides of the Atlantic. By 1917 there were 375 in the United States alone, and that number had risen to over 1600 by 1931. Such independent research firms as that of Arthur D. Little (he once made a silk purse out of a sow's ear, to the delight of the press) undertook contract research to solve industrial problems and, in 1911, helped General Motors establish a lab of its own.

Progress, however, seems still to need genius as well as expertise. At a critical point in Fritz Lang's classic expressionist film *Metropolis* the master of the city visits a half-mad inventor who lives not in one of the shiny skyscrapers of the metropolis but in a tiny wooden dwelling nestled between them, a cottage better suited to the deep woods than the city of the future. The inventor, wild of hair and eye, has a metal hand to replace one amputated in the course of his work; his humanity having been reduced and replaced by the very technology that has destroyed it. The Master has reached a crisis in his relations with his workers and, he tells the inventor, he turns to him for help when his experts fail him.

[14] **Previous page:** Quoted in Archer H. Shaw, ed. *The Lincoln Encyclopedia* (New York: The Macmillan Co., 1950), p. 236.
[15] Friedel, p. 22.

As the neo-liberal economists Jewkes, Sawers and Stillerman pointed out in their 1958 book *The Sources of Invention*, committees don't invent, people do. In a series of charming case studies of twentieth-century invention they show how, time after time, new ideas came from individuals, however necessary large institutions may have been in getting the ideas through to production and market.[16] George Wise has pointed out that new ideas came from people positioned along a spectrum, not clustered at the polar opposites of independent genius and corporate bureaucrat. 'The "outside" inventors', he writes, 'were more dependent on, and the "inside" inventors were more independent of, corporate policies and choices than previous accounts have depicted. Their choice of targets, the marshalling of support, the use of resources and information, differed in degree, not in kind.'[17]

As Edison's experience of inventing a telephone for Western Union shows, even the most 'independent' inventors did contract work for, or sold their ideas to, corporations. At the same time, Wise finds throughout the giant electrical firms 'pockets of invention and innovation', often led by workers who appeared on the official personnel lists as 'shop superintendent', 'consulting engineer', 'mechanical engineer', or under some other job title which did little to reveal their true activities. Such people 'enjoyed the patronage, support, and protection of a high-level executive,' and practised what Wise calls 'intrapreneurship' – 'playing the role of entrepreneur within the corporation'.[18]

Even the stubborn and lavishly-funded resistance of corporations in the law courts to the patent rights of outside inventors sometimes failed to prevent their successful introduction of important new technologies. One of Wise's best stories involves Neils Christensen who was born in Denmark in 1865. After getting some technical education and practical training in his native country, he joined the Danish navy and then jumped ship in Britain, where he went to work for a naval architect at Newcastle-upon-Tyne. Coming to America in 1891, he held several positions; between 1895–99 he patented his first important invention, a braking system for trams which need an air compressor and electric motor, both completely sealed in an oil bath. Beginning in 1905 he spent twenty years battling with the Westinghouse Corporation in the courts over their refusal to acknowledge his patent rights to the device.

Deprived of his reward for his braking device (until 1930, when the courts

[16] John Jewkes, David Sawers and Richard Stillerman, *The Sources of Invention* (New York: St Martin's Press, 1958).

[17] George Wise, 'Inventors and Corporations in the Maturing Electrical Industry, 1890–1940', *Inventive Minds: Creativity in Technology*, ed. Robert J. Weber and David N. Perkins (New York: Oxford University Press, 1992), p. 293.

[18] *Ibid.*, p. 299.

found in his favour), Christensen turned out other inventions, all involving hydraulic or pneumatic power, the fields he knew best. In 1926 the Midvale Steel Products company engaged him to develop automobile and truck brakes for them. In 1933 he came up with his second, and most important, invention – one that would prevent the leaking of fluids around a piston: the O-ring, made tragically famous in 1986 when one failed on the spacecraft *Challenger*.

Wise asserts that 'uncomplicated, functional solutions to common needs are the essence of good design', and the O-ring was a perfect example,[19] A simple rubber ring with the cross-section of a circle, it was designed to fit into a straight-sided groove running around the circumference of a piston. Such arrangements were not uncommon, but the success of Christensen's product lay in the dimensions of the groove – exactly one and a half times the diameter of the ring itself. Christensen had a wrong idea of why it worked so well, but in fact it turned out that the extra room in the groove allowed the ring to roll back and forth, helping to lubricate itself and thus last longer.

The villain of the O-ring story was not a large corporation like Westinghouse, but the United States military. This marks a revealing shift in patronage of technology in the mid-twentieth century. After seven years of lukewarm response from manufacturers, Christensen sold the idea to the military in 1940 as the United States began to gear up its defences for World War II. Each military aircraft had dozens of hydraulic devices for opening bomb bays, raising and lowering wheels, and a myriad other purposes. The Air Corps adopted Christensen's O-rings as standard. When the U.S. finally entered the war, the government bought the rights to many necessary patents, and Christensen received a paltry $75 000 for his. Not until 1964, twelve years after Christensen died, did his estate win a judgement against the government, finally receiving 'reasonable and entire compensation'.

The patent system, which did so much to tempt and frustrate Christensen, has been a divine mystery for two centuries. British monarchs had long made it a habit to grant patents of monopoly to all manner of deserving subjects, from royal creditors to royal favourites (or their husbands). The monopoly on the sale of tea in North America, held by the East India Company, would help to bring on the American Revolution, but discontent with the system was rife at home as well.

[19] George Wise, 'Ring Master',
American Heritage Invention and Technology, 7 (Spring/Summer, 1991), 58.

In 1602, English lawyers argued that: 'when any man by his own charge and industry, or his own wit or invention doth bring any new trade into the realm, or any engine tending to the furtherance of a trade that never was before; and that for the good of the realm; that in such cases the king may grant to him a monopoly-patent for some reasonable time, until the subjects may learn the same, in consideration of the good that he doth bring by his invention to the commonwealth, otherwise not'.[20] Not until 1623, however, was the Parliament able to wring a Statute of Monopolies from a reluctant James I.

The several American colonies tended to follow this practice, though because of the principled opposition to *all* monopolies by the Quaker William Penn, Pennsylvania made no such concession. In 1716, Sybilla Masters, wife of the colony's governor, was forced to apply to Parliament for a patent for her improved mill for 'Cleaning and Curing the Indian Corn Growing in the several colonies of America'. She received her patent, but it was made out to her husband since, as a woman, she could not legally have one herself. Even when Pennsylvania finally did get a Patent Act, the strong tradition of anti-monopoly sometimes prevailed. When urged by another governor to patent his newly-invented, iron heating stove, Benjamin Franklin refused, stating that he 'declined it from a Principle which ever weigh'd with me on such Occasions, viz: That as we enjoy great Advantages from the Invention of others, we should be glad of an Opportunity to serve others by any Invention of ours, and this we should do freely and generously'.[21]

In its Constitution of 1787, the new United States granted to the central government the power to 'promote the Progress of Science and the Useful Arts, by securing for limited Times to Authors and Inventors the exclusive Right to their respective Writings and Discoveries'. Its first patent law, in 1790, set up a committee of three Cabinet officers, headed by Secretary of State Thomas Jefferson, to pass on all patent applications. The task proved too time-consuming for such high officials, and the small number of patents issued under this law, 57 in three years, led inventors to charge Jefferson with being hostile to the mechanic class and forced the writing of a new law in 1793.

The new law was modelled on

Sybilla Masters' Letters of Patent for her improved mill for cleaning and curing Indian corn.

[20] Quoted in Floyd L. Vaughan, *The United States Patent System* (Norman: Univ. of Oklahoma Press, 1956), pp. 14–15.
[21] Benjamin Franklin, *An Account of the Newly Invented Pennsylvania Fire-Place* [1744], ed. Thomas P. Adams (1973), p. v.

Cleaning and Curing Indian Corn.

———————

LETTERS PATENT to Thomas Masters, of Pensilvania, Planter, his Execrs. Adm , and Assignes, of the sole Use and Benefit of " A New Invencon found out by Sybilla his Wife, for Cleaning and Curing the Indian Corn Growing in the severall Colonies in America," within England, Wales, and Town of Berwick-upon-Tweed, and the Colonies in America. Teste R apd Westm̃, 25° die Novrs, anno p̃d.

p brẽ, &c.

Dated 25th November 1715.

that of Britain, requiring only that a statement of originality be sworn and a fee paid. Matters of priority and interference, which proved to be legion, were to be settled by the courts. Finally, in 1836, the world's first modern patent law was passed, setting up a Patent Office with quasi-judicial powers. From then onwards, a patent was *prima facie* evidence of its validity, since every effort was made to confirm its originality and usefulness. Significantly, a system of discriminatory fees was established, making it more expensive for foreigners than American citizens to get patents, and in a category by themselves, most expensive of all for British applicants.

Britain itself reformed its patent law in 1852, to bring it more in line with modern American practice. On both sides of the Atlantic the trick was to protect the rights of the public to new improvements, but at the same time to restrict them sufficiently that inventors would be tempted to disclose the fruits of their genius and thus encourage their rapid diffusion. Giving the inventor a monopoly for a limited number of years was deemed sufficient. The *ancien régime* in France had had a more proactive policy of helping to spread the use of new inventions, but both British and American practice left that to market forces. Over the years there have been frequent attempts to perfect this system, but since there is little clear evidence to show how well it works or why, there has been a conservative tendency to celebrate its presumed efficacy and leave it pretty much alone. Patents, their creation, suppression, avoidance, licensing and litigation have been the mother's milk of corporate technology, and that's the way the game is played.

George Wise has said that in the early twentieth century's 'high-tech' areas of development – alternating current electricity and the radio, for example – the scientific training American engineers received in university placed them at a distinct advantage. As early as 1894 the journal *Scientific American* had complained that 'those who pursue electricity, by the inductive method – that of practical experiment and generalization therefrom – have lately entered the complaint that electricity has become nine-tenths mathematics. To many real experimental discoverers, the higher branches of mathematics constitute a trackless maze'.[22]

On the other hand 'when it came to mechanical systems', Wise concludes, 'the European-born, shop-trained craftsmen-engineers still designed rings around their college-trained yankee rivals'.[23] Eugene Ferguson sounded a warning about the loss of this same practical, commonsense, understanding of how things work.

[22] 'The Potentialities of Chemical Research', *Scientific American*, 70 (20 January 1894), 34.
[23] Wise, 'Inventors' p. 303.

While it is true that the high-tech field has expanded exponentially over the past half-century, and while it is true that the practical approach is still necessary for avoiding potentially costly and dangerous design mistakes, a firm grasp of science is equally important for understanding both problems and solutions. While technology in general cannot be reduced to simply 'applied science', there are increasing cases where quite recent developments in science have found their way into various applications. The laser is a case in point.

Quantum physics is a field which, before the Second World War, had a certain popular cachet from its association with the work of Albert Einstein, but had produced little in the form of useful technology. Since the War, spin off from this research has produced devices from the atomic bomb to the semiconductor. The laser (Light Amplification by Stimulated Emission of Radiation) also came from the field of quantum physics. Wartime research, especially efforts to improve radar, was critical. Early in the war, British radar operated with microwaves of 10 centimetres, but it was realized that shorter waves would improve operation of the device. After the War, scientists interested in investigating radiation absorption by molecules realized that they too needed to generate microwaves with wavelengths in the millimetre range.

One of the early players was Charles Hard Townes who, in 1951, was a professor of physics at Columbia University in New York City and Director of the Columbia Radiation Laboratory. Townes, in many ways, showed all the characteristics of an American inventor in the last half of the twentieth century. He had taken his university degrees in physics but during the war had worked essentially as an engineer, designing radar bombing systems at Bell Laboratories. After the war he went to Columbia, but also worked for the Office of Naval Research. In his associations, therefore, he almost defined the new mix of military/industrial/academic power that US President Dwight Eisenhower warned against in his farewell address to the nation.

At Columbia, as director of a laboratory, Townes had access not only to military funding but graduate students and academic colleagues. One of his research associates, Arthur L. Schawlow, who also married Townes's sister, went to work for AT&T's Bell Laboratories. Townes was himself a consultant at Bell, the two began working together again and in 1958 applied for a patent on behalf

of Bell. Other researchers in the field had similar affiliations. Robert H. Dicke, for example, who made notes on an infra-red laser in 1956, worked at Princeton University and for RCA.

R. Gordon Gould was a graduate student at Columbia who had worked a while as an independent inventor, and still thought of himself that way. After leaving Columbia he went to work for TRG, Inc. where he pursued his laser project with a million-dollar grant from the US Department of Defense's Advanced Research Projects Agency (ARPA). It was a good time to secure military patronage. In October 1957 the Soviet Union had put into orbit the first artificial satellite, *Sputnik*, and a frightened and embarrassed United States was prepared to spend big money to catch up.

The physical principle behind the laser was that 'an excited atom releases radiation of a specific wavelength when it is acted upon by radiation of the same wavelength', as Joan Lisa Bromberg, the historian of the laser, explains.[24] The problem lay in its parts: what kind of atoms to use, for example, and how to excite them. By 1962 some 400 companies had laser projects going. That same year the military spent US $12 million supporting laser research, and in 1963 spent US $20 million. In this, as in so many areas of recent technology, the role of the military as patron of research and development can hardly be overestimated.

Townes shared the 1964 Nobel Prize in physics with two Soviet pioneers, but, as it turned out, he was not in the final sprint for a commercially practical laser. Some years earlier he had taken a leave of absence from Columbia to be director of research for the Institute for Defense Analysis (which was an advisory body to the Pentagon's ARPA), and in 1961 he became provost of MIT. R. Gordon Gould, too, was not in at the kill. His work at TRG was so important to the military they made it classified information, then banned Gould from working on it further because he had belonged to a Marxist study group during the Second World War. Military patronage was a two-edged weapon; it could prevent as well as enhance technological development and personal careers.

Both Townes and Gould had contributed greatly to the eventual success of the laser, but did so in interestingly different ways. As Bromberg has pointed out, Townes approached his work as a scientist, using 'materials that were well understood and would yield simple, predictable results'. He wanted to perfect

A researcher wears a protective visor to conduct a high speed Neodymium yttrium-aluminium-garnet (Nd-YAG) laser beam.

[24] Joan Lisa Bromberg, 'Amazing Light', *American Heritage Invention and Technology*, 7 (Spring, 1992), p. 18.

techniques and explain results more than he wanted to build a useful device. He was far from the popular notion of an other-worldly, 'pure' scientist, but he was deeply religious, and 'saw basic science as a means of approaching sacred truths'.

Gould, on the other hand, had always thought of himself as an inventor, and picked up his Ph.D to gain the background (and perhaps the social authority) he needed to be successful. As Bromberg notes, 'within a year of first conceiving of the laser he had mapped out many different ways one could be built, explored scores of possible media and methods of excitation, and suggested applications by the dozen, some of which would be put into practice years later'.[25]

And those applications are both varied and ubiquitous. The laser's beam of light is used to play compact discs, direct 'smart bombs', perform eye surgery, guide tractors in levelling rice fields, print computer files and for innumerable other tasks. One increasingly common use illustrates the convergence of different technologies into new systems: laser is used to read the bar codes on products in shops and in many other applications. So common is this use of lasers, that when President George Bush failed to recognize it while visiting a supermarket during his election campaign, his ignorance was taken as a sign that he had lost touch with the experience of ordinary people. How the bar code developed reveals a great deal about the relationship between inventors and industry.

In 1948, Bernard Silver, a graduate student at Philadelphia's Drexel Institute of Technology, overheard an executive of a food company express the need for a device to gather automatically product information at the checkout. Silver dropped out of college and, with the help of another student, Norman Woodland, combined key elements from the Morse code and Lee de Forest's 1920s movie sound system. Silver extended Morse's dots and dashes vertically, then read them with the movie projector apparatus. He soon (mistakenly as it turned out), changed the vertical marks to a bull's-eye arrangement, and they filed for a patent in 1949.

Woodland later went to work for IBM and hoped to perfect their technology, but two problems made the task difficult. In their system paper carrying the code was moved in front of a strong light. The beams reflected were fed into a photo-multiplier tube that is generally used to pick up the soundtrack on motion picture films, and the resulting pulse recorded on an oscilloscope. How best to produce the light, and what to do with the information gathered were problems crying out

[25] Bromberg, pp. 25–26.

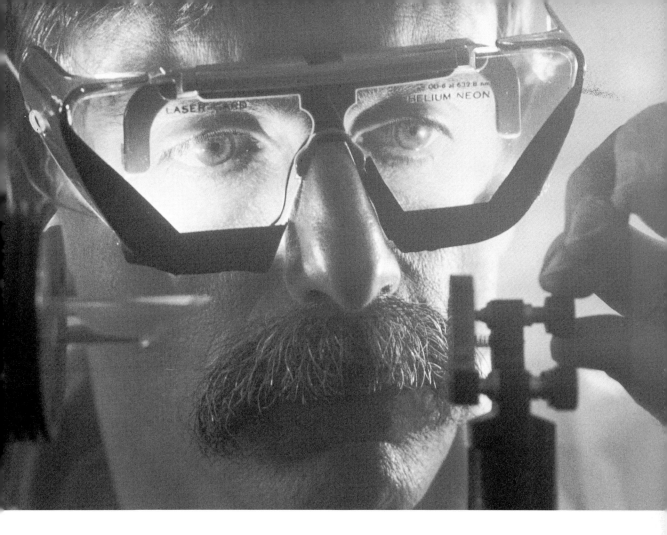

for the laser and the computer, but since the latter was not yet useful for the purpose and the former hardly invented, other steps had to be taken. Philco radio bought the patent rights to the system in 1962 and later sold them to RCA.

About the same time David J. Collins, a former MIT graduate working at the Sylvania Corporation, worked out a code of coloured dots which could be arranged to represent the digits 0–9. He had once worked for a railway company, and successfully convinced one to fit the code in its carriages in 1961. As the carriages entered the yard, a reader identified them by scanning the dots with coloured lights. Collins then quit Sylvania, set up his own firm, and began at last to use lasers to scan a bar code.

Above: checking a helium/neon laser of the US National Institute of Standards and Technology-7 atomic clock. The laser counts the oscillations of excited hydrogen ions held within an ion trap. Counting the oscillations is the key to the extreme accuracy of the NIST-7.

Since the black bars absorbed the light and the white spaces reflected it, he received a simple off/on signal.

Meanwhile RCA, with the patents of Silver and Woodland, returned to the grocery industry for a market. An industry consortium agreed on uniform standards, but the bull's-eye code proved difficult to read. At IBM Woodland worked out the now dominant Universal Product Code (UPC). The UPC was adopted in 1973, and on 26 June 1974 a pack of chewing gum sold in Troy, Ohio, became 'the first retail product sold with the help of a scanner'.[26] In 1978, in the United States, less than one per cent of grocery stores had scanners; by 1981 it was ten per cent; by 1984, thirty-three per cent and in 1993 more than sixty per cent.

Woodland also developed the European Article Numbering system (EAN), which has an extra pair of digits and is rapidly becoming the world standard. The technology represents a massive leap forward in digitalized control – bar codes are used to keep track of tins of soup, marathon runners, the mating habits of bees, and logs in lumber yards. The grocery checkout laser/bar-code system not only records the price of the product, it keeps track of the efficiency of the checkout worker, of the store's inventory, and, when combined with payment by credit card, provides demographic data on customers and their consumption patterns. 'This thing is a success story on the American way of doing things', said Alan

Above left: a supermarket checkout counter showing the bar-code reader in use. Above right: an example of the bar codes now found on most products.

[26] Tony Seideman, 'Bar Codes Sweep the World', *American Heritage Invention and Technology*, 8 (Spring, 1993), 63.

Haberman, president of First National Stores. 'Our own initiative – take it on ourselves, inviting the world to join in. It has something to say about the little guys with lots of vision'.[27]

It is not clear which 'little guys' Haberman was referring to, since the manufacturing and marketing power of IBM, and the formal standardization of the entire grocery industry were as necessary for the success of barcodes as was the inventive talent of Silver, Collins and Woodland. The fact is that while invention is almost by definition something new coming from outside the existing system, and inventors have frequently flourished best when allowed to work outside a system, being on the margin *per se* can be as destructive as inspiring.

The inventors and engineers of the Industrial Revolution tended to come from the margins rather than the centre of British society, but the labouring proletariat was not a fruitful source of new technologies. The new United States, cut off politically and geographically from the 'workshop of the world', proved a fertile source of new and basic inventions during the nineteenth century, but these seem to have come mostly from the nation's cities, not the western frontier – from white artisans and mechanics, not from black slaves.

And no women anywhere in the Atlantic community made contributions to invention and engineering design to any degree in comparison to their numbers. They were systematically marginalized as far as technological, or any other kind of power, was concerned. Barred from machine shops and engineering institutions, to a large extent from higher education, and told that they lacked the proper mental and emotional endowments for dealing creatively with technology, they were accepted as machine tenders, and increasingly as machine purchasers, but not as designers and inventors.

'Out-of-the-Loop', therefore, was a fact of life and perhaps even an advantage for many inventors, but it was clearly possible to get too far outside the sustaining orbit of power. For every poet who languished, unappreciated, there was an inventor with a vision no one would share, or a scheme in which only she or he had faith. An eighteenth-century American steamboat inventor did well to call his last, unfinished vessel the *Perseverance*. It was a virtue necessary but not sufficient for success. Successful invention has been shown to be a rich but unstable mixture of genius and expertise, luck and planning, independence and compulsion.

[27] Quoted in Seideman, p. 63.

Chapter three

STEP RIGHT UP

■ *Time is so not everything happens at once.*
Space is so everything doesn't happen to you.

GRAFFITO

An early 'motion' picture by Marey.

ECHNOLOGY, IN ONE SENSE, is the way in which we organize ourselves and our environment – it is creative in that it gives definition to what was already present, but inchoate. In modern times this has frequently taken the form of rationalization, imposing a form or pattern on things or events. It is tempting to divide the past into pre-modern, modern, and post-modern periods on the basis of how time and space have been organized. The pre-industrial rhythms of season and day, cycles of birth, maturity and death, the flow of work from beginning to end, all suggest a wheel of life, marked off in stages but always returning upon itself. Space too had its local meanings, and the sense of locality was sufficient to include and define birth and death, labour and love.

It was a mark of the modern, however, to divide things into identical units which could be both sequenced and quantified. The clocking of time, the mapping of land, the division of labour, and the counting of everything led to a different understanding and use of people and things. This sort of standardization and rationalization reached its culmination, perhaps, in the work of Frederick Winslow Taylor in the early years of this century. His system of 'Scientific Management' attempted to discover the natural 'laws' which governed all human activity so that people as well as machines could be interchangeable. It was equally a mark of modernism to define a metropolis against its periphery, to subordinate the edge to the centre, depriving locality of both competence and meaning.

Similarly, it is a mark of the post-modern era (if, indeed, such a thing exists) that time and space have not so much been sequenced as obliterated. Compared to the modernist ideal, the process has been valued over the product, the difference between periphery and centre dissolved, and the reader considered more important than the text. Distinctions once thought clear and immutable are being broken down or, what amounts to the same thing, redefined. Such relied-upon bipolar concepts as private/public, life/death, human/machine, here/there, now/then, are rapidly losing their usefulness in making meaningful distinctions. If most of our understanding is based upon coordinates of time and space, the obliteration of those two landmarks has profound cultural consequences.

Our experience of time, for example, has changed vastly over the millennia.

The metaphor of time as a river flowing endlessly on, seamless and unidirectional, captures the notion that time is natural, a part of nature, and to be experienced in the flow of natural events. The rising and setting of the sun, the seasonal needs of agriculture, the birth and death of generations, all mark the natural 'passing' of time (as if by a point fixed in space). It was an understanding nicely expressed in the water-clocks of ancient China, the finest instruments of their time.

Medieval Europe, however, came up with a different, mechanical, clock, that profoundly changed the possibilities and the perception of measured time. This new clock was made up of three distinct but connected parts: weights which in falling provided the power for the device; a gear train which could transmit the energy provided by the weights; and a measuring mechanism which marked the passing of time. It was this last component that was the most powerful break-through in clock design. Although time was seen as flowing endlessly, the best way to trace that flow was to break it into identical bits which could be counted.

Thus the rocking escape mechanism that alternately allowed and prevented the flow of energy from the weights, turning a wheel, provided a near-perfect device for dividing time into beats. This go-no-go device was remarkably analogous to that family of technology that includes gauges for precision machine work and the functioning of modern computers. The escape mechanism not only allowed time to be broken into discrete bits, it sent these to any one of a number of devices which could keep track of and display this information: the hands on the clock face, bells to be struck at appropriate times, and so forth. Finally, by breaking the fall of the weights for a time, the escapement lengthened the time it would operate without having to be raised again or, when weights came to be replaced by springs, to be wound.

It is generally true that the smaller the segments into which time is divided, the faster the beat, and the more accurate the counting of time. Mechanical clocks of the early four-teenth century often had beats which lasted several seconds. By about 1800 clocks gen-erally managed two beats a second; today a good quartz watch will produce more than

Figures of life and death on the wheel of fortune shown in Medieval English literature.

LAP·SPLIT MEMORY

1/1000 SECOND

CASIO

LAP·SPL MEMORY

LAP·SPLIT / RESET

LIGHT

TMR MODE

TR-1 TR-2 TR-3

24HR

START·STOP

ADJUST / TIMER SEL.

STW REC ALM

LAP SPL

LED INDICATOR

JAPAN

SIST 100M

100 000 beats per second. The atomic clocks used by astronomers today, however, operate at over 9 billion cycles per second. This kind of precision is far beyond the need and financial resources of the common person.

The earliest mechanical clocks, like the atomic clocks of today, were for public purposes and produced what can be thought of as public time. Whether on a church tower or the town hall, it imposed a public discipline, marking not only precisely but authoritatively the hours of prayer and commerce. This public standard of time now made possible, perhaps even inevitable, the notions of productivity and efficiency, discipline and rationality. Samuel Butler's *Erehwon* (1872) is a novel set in a dystopia where the clock has been banned. This act marks that point in history (that is, in time) when machines have reached a stage beyond which they will become a threat rather than a resource.

One signal characteristic of the mechanical clock was that it was self-contained and therefore, in theory, capable of being miniaturized and made portable. It was 500 years before the pocket and wrist watch converted *public* to *private* time, but the transformation was profound. As the historian David Landes has pointed out, 'it was this possibility of widespread private use that laid the basis for *time discipline*, as against *time obedience*. One can ... use public clocks to summon people for one purpose or another; but that is not punctuality. Punctuality comes from within, not from without.'[1]

So deeply did this sense of being a 'timely' people penetrate the European consciousness that when they began to explore the 'new' worlds, the different concept of time of the indigenous people became a measure of their worthlessness. Not surprisingly, most scored poorly by this European test, giving invading powers yet another excuse for exploitation. Even at home, as the Industrial Revolution began to change the ways in which people worked, punctuality became a marker of character and respectability.

Something of the ideology of clocks can be understood by comparing them with another critical technology, that of feedback mechanisms which monitor and adjust the actions of other devices. Such mechanisms were known in ancient times and during the flowering of Islamic culture, that is, up until the end of the twelfth century. They were ignored in Europe from the Middle Ages until the Industrial Revolution, when they reappeared in Britain. In *Authority, Liberty & Automatic*

Casio sports watch. Far left: a Chinese water clock. Left: Su Sung's mechanical water clock.

[1] David S. Landes, *Revolution in Time: Clocks and the Making of the Modern World* (Cambridge: Harvard Univ. Press, 1983), p. 7.

Machinery in Early Modern Europe the historian of technology Otto Mayr asks
why feedback should be revived in Britain at that time, while continuing to be
ignored on the continent of Europe.[2]

His answer is obvious and surprising. Continental technology tended towards
the monumental, the dramatic and the ingenious. Great clocks and a staggering
array of incredibly intricate automata, lifelike figures and scenes driven by
clockwork, fit nicely into this prejudice. Feedback, on the other hand, works quietly
and anonymously, an unimpressive part of some larger machine. Furthermore, as
Mayr argues, the clock was the perfect symbol of authority and stability, political
and intellectual criteria much admired in Europe. Feedback, on the other hand,
was a balancing mechanism, allowing well-regulated liberty rather than imposing
a central authority. Such mechanisms, indeed, made their appearance at about
the same time that Sir Isaac Newton was proposing a solar system of balanced,
planetary forces, Adam Smith a balanced economy of market forces, and a host
of politicians a liberal polity of checks and balances. James Watt's celebrated
governor to regulate the workings of his improved steam engine was, in fact, a
fitting technological symbol of his age.

Each era seemed to find its own needs for the closer regulation of time. The
building of railways in the nineteenth century placed new premiums on timetables
and precision. The times when trains left, arrived, and most importantly passed
each other, became matters literally of life and death. The invention of the electric
telegraph by Samuel F.B. Morse in the United States led to its use in 1837 on the
London and North-Western Railway, thus making possible precisely identical time
readings at stations throughout the system. A decade later the British Railway
Clearing House recommended that all British railways adopt Greenwich time for
their operations.

All modernizing nations faced the same problems of coordinating railway
time, but the United States (and later Russia) had particular difficulty because of
the vast distances encompassed by their tracks. In 1883, American railway
companies agreed on a partition of the country into four time zones and this led
to international agreements to divide the entire world into such zones. Greenwich
was accepted as the basic starting point by all but France, which wanted Paris to
be the starting point and which held out until 1911. The imperialism of railway

[2] Otto Mayr, *Authority, Liberty &*
Automatic Machinery in Early Modern
Europe (Baltimore: Johns Hopkins
University Press, 1986).

time over local times was resisted in some places. God's plan in having the sun directly overhead at noon was being rudely and impiously pushed aside by a new, mechanical, human and profit-driven method of dividing the day, and the outrage did not go unmarked.

Two lines of development have marked the evolution of clocks, at least over the past two centuries. First was the attempt to make them less expensive so that every adult could (and would want to) carry one. The American System of Manufactures, perfected in the United States federal armouries during the first half of the nineteenth century, was quickly applied to watch and clock making. Dedicated precision machine tools, and the use of jigs, fixtures and gauges to ensure uniformity, allowed producers to turn out large quantities of identical pieces at an ever-reducing cost. The apotheosis of mass-produced watches appeared in 1949 when the Timex watch was first produced. By 1960 the Timex company was producing 8 million of them a year and by the early 1970s, 30 million pieces in plants all around the world. Timepieces were sold so cheaply that they were discarded rather than repaired when they broke down.

The other great industry desideratum was increased accuracy. As we have noted, accuracy was best achieved through the division of time into smaller and smaller segments which translated into faster and faster beats. At the turn of the

The departures board at Waterloo Station in London.

century Pierre Curie noticed that certain crystals vibrated mechanically when subjected to an alternating electric current. The first clock using a quartz crystal was built in the 1920s, and the first quartz clock was installed at Greenwich in 1939. It was always the astronomers who most wanted the more exact time such pieces could deliver.

In 1960 the Bulova Accutron, with an oscillating tuning-fork replacing the ancient balance wheel and hairspring for controller, went on the market. The Japanese firm Seiko brought out its first electronic watch in 1968–69, and in 1969 the Hamilton Watch Company in the United States came out with the Pulsar, the first all-electronic watch that had a digital display rather than conventional face with hands (or analogue dial). David Landes rhapsodizes that 'a good movement, especially a complicated one, has art and grace and life', adding, 'it is hard to love a quartz timepiece'.[3] For those so inclined, it is a sad realization that not only has the quartz watch conquered all (but hearts), it is certainly not the last word in accuracy because of the quest for ever-finer splitting of time.

Not only time, but space too must be divided in order to be used. In the spring of 1993 it was possible to buy a device to carry in one's pocket which could communicate through a satellite and indicate location on the earth within 100 feet. Apparently it could be even more accurate, but for the fact that the United States defence services wanted to keep the signal fuzzy for security purposes. Why anyone outside a James Bond film might need to know her or his position with that degree of accuracy is not clear. We are told that the technology would help us find our way to our vehicle in the car park, but such modern 'needs' hardly seem as pressing as those which led to the sequencing of space in the first place.

Presumably people in all ages have had a need to know more or less where they were, though the reference point must have varied widely. Australian Aborigines used decorated marking sticks as well as the reservoir of stories of the Dreamtime to help them navigate the vast reaches of the outback that was their home. The Star of Bethlehem guided the Magi, and land deeds from colonial America define property boundaries as 'northerly to the big rock, thence east to the blasted oak. ...' The latter description is, in its way, the spatial equivalent of getting up with the chickens and going to bed with the sun.

The Romans, with their monumental technologies and imperial desires, found

---

[3] Landes, p. 352.

the need for a more formal and abstract system of measurement. The *passus* (about two ordinary paces) served to link nearness (as in agriculture) and farness (as in distant encampments or colonies). The *mille*, the *stadium* and other measures knit together the vast area encompassed by the Roman Empire. As the historian Hunter Dupree explains, this scale became embedded in English practice and tradition through the Roman occupation of Britain. When Edward I (or II, the date is unclear) ordered that three 'barley-corns, round and dry, make an inch, twelve inches make a foot, three feet a yard, five and a half yards a perch [or rod], and forty perches in length and four in breadth an acre', he was codifying both practice and tradition. Medieval farmers ploughed the length of the acre, troubling themselves to turn the plough and team of oxen as infrequently as possible.

The linking of what Dupree terms 'bench marks' – the anatomical standards of finger, thumb, hand and foot which were of particular use to artisans – through the rod, furlong and acre of the farmer, to the miles that interested the trader, soldier and sovereign, was one of the great intellectual feats of western civilization.

One dramatic extension of this system occurred in 1785 when the new confederation of American states decided to order a survey of its newly acquired western lands mapped on a grid in sections of one square mile. Just as the acre of medieval England is etched on the land today, so the 1785 grid which moved westward across the United States as the nation expanded is a visible feature for all people travelling by air in that country today. The grid is burned into the politics and economics of the nation as well. A square mile (one section) contains 640 acres. One quarter (160 acres) was the homestead given free by the government to new settlers in the West. A quarter of that, or 40 acres, along with a mule was the symbol and for many the reality of subsistence living.

The survey, both for exploration and for mapping, was one of the great adventures of the late eighteenth and nineteenth centuries. Nations with an internal empire, like the United States, or an overseas one, like Great Britain, used the survey as a tool of imperial rule, replacing the local knowledge of indigenous peoples with a central rationality imposed by the occupying power. The great British survey of India served this purpose, by its very precision invoking a power beyond the means or understanding of the local populations.

In the United States the grid survey, like the marking of time by clocks, promoted the quantifying of what had been to some extent a common experience. An acre, of equal size and shape to any other of its kind, and almost infinitely capable of division or multiplication, could more readily be bought and sold. Property in this sense was unknown to the indigenous Americans who held historic rights of contingent use to certain places, but little more. Objects or possessions intended to be articles of commerce were best divided into formal and inter-changeable parts – just, indeed, as was money itself.

The division and placing in sequence of time and space found a new imperative in the Industrial Revolution. Work was one such area of intensification. Adam Smith's description of the 'division of labour' in the manufacture of pins has become a classic, but the widening use of machines greatly extended the process. Among artisans, it was still common for the master, with the help of journeyman and apprentice, to make individual pieces, performing all the steps and taking full responsibility for the product.

What came to be called the American System of Manufactures, or more accurately 'armoury practice', had precedents in the manufacture of naval blocks (the wooden frames which held the pulleys over which ropes passed) in Britain, of clocks in Sweden, and small arms in France. It was in America, however, that it was most fully worked out and applied. Special machine tools were designed to make large numbers of interchangeable parts; since the skill and tolerances were now built into the machines, unskilled or semi-skilled labour could be applied. It was not true mass production yet because assembly was still done in the traditional, static way, but each worker at a separate machine now worked on a different part.

The United States Commissioner of Labor reported in 1898 that machines had replaced manual processes to such an extent that only by moving away from modern methods in time and space could the older methods be recaptured. A survey interviewed elderly and retired workers and visited shops in small towns far from the centres of production. The comparison of how things were done in the past and the present revealed dramatic advances in the division of labour during the middle years of the nineteenth century.

One example will suffice. Men's 'cheap grade, kip, pegged boots, half-double soles' had been made by hand in 1859 and machine in 1895. In 1859 making 100 pairs by hand involved 83 separate operations. By 1895 this had been divided into

122. More significantly, the number of workers employed had increased from 2 to 113! The hours worked, however, under this new division of labour and machine operation, fell from about 1436 to 154, and the cost of labour dropped from US $408 to US $35.[4] The relentless drive to rationalize the use of labour had not yet reached the excesses of the Ford assembly line of the early twentieth century, but the direction of change was obvious – and ominous.

The division of labour was not the only way in which that factor of production was measured during the early years of the Industrial Revolution. Eugene S. Ferguson has chronicled the effort of scientists, from the late seventeenth century onwards, to measure the 'Man-Days' involved in work. In 1637 Descartes had already declared that the animal machine, as 'made by the hands of God, [was] incomparably better ordered [and] more admirable in its movements than any of those which can be invented by men'.[5] Not content with this distinction, scientists made repeated attempts to measure human work and calculate therefrom a standard 'Man-Day' which could, presumably, be expected of anyone.

Above: 'Clocking on' at work. Employees' working hours were monitored by the machine which recorded their arrival and departure times on a card.

[4] *Thirteenth Annual Report of the Commissioner of Labor. 1898. Hand and Machine Labor*, Vol. 1 (Washington, 1899), p. 28–29.
[5] Quoted in Anson Rabinbach, *The Human Motor: Energy, Fatigue, and the Origins of Modernity* (New York: Basic Books, 1990), p. 1.

The effort began perhaps with Giovanni Borelli who attempted to calculate the working of the human machine by adding the efforts of each 'lever and cord' at work in a single body. Most of his successors decided to treat the body as a single machine, rather than a collection of machines. Beginning with Philippe de la Hire in 1699, a whole series of investigators tried to compare how much work people could do compared to a horse – vague estimates, wild prejudice and peculiar analogies abounded. An English lecturer in 1734 asserted that while it took only five Englishmen to equal the work of one horse, it would require seven Frenchmen or Dutchmen to do the same amount. When James Watt chose a work rating for his steam engine in terms of 'horsepower', the term became detached from the animal and from humans: 'manpower' became a separate subject of study.

Over the next two centuries the subjects of experiments carried loads up stairways, polished pieces of glass, turned wheels and undertook other tasks. All these activities were measured, estimated or assessed by guess-work to produce a standard of 'manpower'. Late in the eighteenth century the French engineer and physicist Charles Augustin de Coulomb saw a young man climbing a steep stairway and noted that it took him twenty minutes to climb about 150 metres. Coulomb offered him money to try to repeat the climb eighteen times in six hours. The young man refused, stating quite sensibly that 'he would not only become exhausted but also be laughed at for climbing the same stairway 18 times in a day'.[6] James Watt once had described to him a rocking-beam water pump that was powered by a young man who ran back and forth from one end to the other for ten hours a day. Since he weighed only 135 lb he was required to carry a 30 lb weight with him to increase the output. Using Coulomb's formula, the man was doing a day's work of 553 000 kilogram-metres.

The concept and use of 'manpower' was not only cruel and degrading, it was also inefficient. Ferguson has calculated that the workers at the London docks, movingly described by Henry Mayhew in 1861, produced the equivalent of only one kilowatt-hour of mechanical energy per head per day. He also points out that the undeniable efficiencies produced by the scientific management investigators of the early twentieth century were primarily based not on these earlier attempts to measure workers *as* machines, but rather as *parts* of machines – as machine tenders and servers. Either way, as C.S. Lewis noted, 'what we call Man's power over

[6] Eugene S. Ferguson, 'The Measurement of the "Man-Day",' *Scientific American*, 225 (October, 1971), 99.

76

Nature turns out to be a power exercised by some men over other men with Nature as its instrument'.[7]

A distant cousin of this early experimentation is the modern science of ergonomics, which can be defined as the attempt to study people in order better to adapt machines to human capabilities. Industrial design, psychology and orthopaedic medicine all make their contributions. Using such techniques as time-lapse photography and prototype devices fitted out with electronic probes, investigators are trying, for example, to redesign the office chair so that people who spend a workday in front of a computer do not develop repetitive strain injuries and the other painful and crippling problems associated with sitting for long periods repeating a few simple movements.

A better chair, some believe, is one solution to the problem, and a debate has developed between chair manufacturers, who want to keep chairs simple for purposes of more efficient production, and ergonomic designers who are advocating individually adjustable chairs with 150 parts accompanied by a manual for the owners. The fidgeting of pupils that generations of schoolteachers have attempted to suppress is called 'micromovement' by the ergonomics people, and the ergonomic chair is designed to accomplish a similar kind of fidget-free seating.[8]

In very recent times the urge to subject people to the nice distinctions of science has resulted in a massive genome mapping and sequencing project, headquartered in the United States but including scientists across the globe. The genetically coded DNA molecule in the human being is made up of some 3 billion base pairs (bp). These occur in a certain order and carry all the genetic information possessed by an individual. The goal, likened by some scientists to the project to put astronauts on the moon, is to produce a physical map of the genome, identifying and showing exactly where in the sequence each of the 3 billion pairs resides. In 1990 it was estimated that it cost between three and five US dollars to sequence each bp. However, technology being developed, especially in Japan, would drastically cut costs by automating the process.

The dream behind the project was a model of the Enlightenment Project – that is, the effort to perfect the world through deliberate and rational action. James D. Watson, co-discoverer with Francis Crick of the double helix structure of DNA in 1953, insists that the pay-off would be 'far greater' than that of the

[7] Quoted in Ferguson, 103.
[8] *New York Times*, 7 July 1992.

moon landing. 'A more important set of instruction books will never be found by human beings,' he wrote in 1990. 'When finally interpreted, the genetic messages encoded within our DNA molecules will provide the ultimate answers to the chemical underpinnings of human existence. They will not only help us understand how we function as healthy human beings, but will also explain, at the chemical level, the role of genetic factors in a multitude of human diseases. . . .'[9]

The dream of understanding better what makes people 'tick' and the chance of mitigating human suffering are both powerful motives behind this effort to reduce people to their smallest meaningful parts. Two more problematic issues lie only slightly below the surface. The least alarming, but still worrisome, is the commercial monopoly of applications of the genome map: the making of profit from the creation of new drugs and procedures and the marketing of new forms of life. Even more sinister is the stimulus this would surely give to the endemic dream of engineering 'superior' people, and a new standard by which 'inferior' people might be judged. Watson himself suggested that three per cent of funds for the project be spent on researching the ethical and social implications of the knowledge he hopes to develop. Citing the horrors of Nazi atrocities, he warned in 1990 that 'if we fail to act now, we might witness unwanted and unnecessary abuses that eventually will create a strong popular backlash against the human genetics community'.[10]

The technological transformation of time and space in the industrial age found its cultural expression in new efforts in art, science, literature and philosophy. They attempted to depict and understand these fundamental principles, now cut loose from old certainties and traditional meanings. The photograph, that copy of reality made possible via industrialization, proved instructively difficult, especially when it came to recording motion. Early critics acknowledged the merit of the photograph in recording architecture and other 'scenes', but denied that it could ever capture 'life' in all its disparate activity. But motion, after all, was the melding of time and space, and before it could be 'captured' it had to be broken down into discrete 'still' pictures, much as time had to be divided by hours and minutes, and space by miles and feet.

In 1859, however, George Washington Wilson shot very fast photographs of pedestrians on the streets of Edinburgh and Edward Anthony took similar scenes

[9] James D. Watson, 'The Human Genome Project: Past, Present, and Future', *Science*, 248 (6 April 1990), 44.
[10] *Ibid.*, 46.

Examples of Edward Muybridge's fast speed photographs from his eleven-volume work, *Animal Locomotion.*

of New York. The remarkable thing about these pictures was that they did *not* show any motion; the obviously moving vehicles and figures were not at all blurred. In America, Oliver Wendell Holmes, concerned in 1863 with the design of artificial limbs for wounded Civil War soldiers, found the pictures of people frozen in mid-step 'a new source' of information about how people really walked.

Ten years later Leland Stanford, a former governor of California, hired Eadweard Muybridge to photograph his prize race horse, 'Occident', while the latter was trotting. The photographer expressed doubt that it could be done. A colourful character, Muybridge (born Edward Muggeridge in Kingston-on-Thames in Britain in 1830) experimented with a series of camera arrangements and new lens shutters until he was able to get clear (fast) shots of the animal. His experiments were interrupted by his trial for murdering his wife's lover (he was acquitted), but resumed in 1877. Muybridge's successful pictures showed for the first time that the trotter did indeed have all four feet off the ground at once, but

A phonograph and kinetoscope parlour in America.

only when they were drawn together under the belly. He also proved that the 'hobbyhorse' position, with front legs extended forward and hind legs stretched to the rear, never occurred, though it was enshrined in innumerable paintings dear to horse fanciers.

Muybridge went on to take a great number of fast speed photographs of all sorts of animals and of people – nude and draped, fencing, walking, jumping, laying bricks, climbing stairs and so forth. They were published in an eleven-volume work, *Animal Locomotion*. It was his intention that it should serve as a 'visual dictionary' of living forms in action.

When the journal *Scientific American* published the pictures in 1878, it invited readers to cut them out, mount them on a 'zoetrope', a popular toy which, when twirled, would produce a 'moving picture'. Since the eye retains an image for a short but sufficient length of time, a new one presented before the former image has faded creates the illusion of motion. Two years later Muybridge used a larger but similar device to project a rapid sequence of slides before an audience at the California School of Fine Arts. He is as good a candidate as any other to stake a claim to the first motion picture, since the 'movies' of today work in essentially the same way.

Thomas Edison's 'Kinetoscope' was the first motion picture system to gain wide popularity. Photographs were taken and projected at the rate of about 48 a second. An electric motor propelled the film which was placed between a light bulb and a rotating disk with a slot for its edge. A Kinetoscope parlour with ten of these machines opened in New York in 1894 and, although only one person at a time could view them through the eyepieces, the entertainment was a great success. The celebrated Cinematographe of the French brothers, Louis and Auguste Lumière, became the first widely successful system, in 1895, to project the moving pictures against a screen so that an entire audience could enjoy it together. Within a year a number of systems were showing films in all the principal cities of Europe and America.

It was not the entertainment potential of Muybridge's work, however, that interested Etienne-Jules Marey, the French physiologist and *savant*. Born in 1830, he had wanted to become an engineer but bowed to his father's wishes and trained to become a physician instead. During his distinguished career as a researcher,

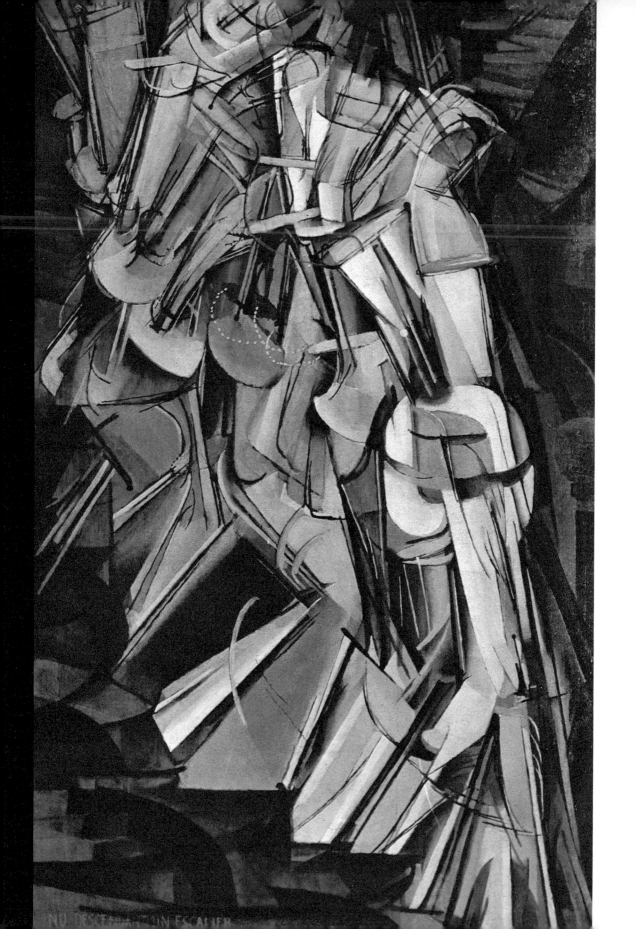

however, he combined his early love and his professional training in the study of 'movement' in what he called the 'animal machine'. He became, as one student said, 'an engineer of life.' Entranced by the idea that 'the body is a theatre of motion', Marey, too, turned to the running horse as a proper subject of study.[11] Using 'inscriptors' attached to the horse's hooves, while the rider used a portable 'inscriptive apparatus', Marey was able to record electrically a graphic depiction of the horse's gait.

When Marey saw Muybridge's photographs, he immediately realized their superiority to the drawing based on his own instrument readings. He was disappointed, however, that time was absent from Muybridge's results. Anson Rabinbach notes, 'as Muybridge had successfully achieved the decomposition of motion, after 1882 Marey pursued the more elusive decomposition of motion into time.'[12] His richly inventive mind finally came up with a method of including a clock face with a luminous dial in the pictures taken, thus providing for the inclusion of time into motion studies.

Marey's own studies now seem hopelessly enmeshed in the nineteenth-century attempts to make a 'science of man', but two other innovators, concerned with the same problems, picked up his work and carried it in different directions. Frank Gilbreth, a contemporary of Frederick Winslow Taylor – the 'Father' of Scientific Management – achieved his reputation in the field of time and motion studies on the careful filming of people at work, with a clock in the corner of the frame to mark the time elapsed. The movements thus recorded were then broken down into therbligs (Gilbreth almost spelt backwards), his name for the basic units of bodily action.

Another successor to Marey was the artist Marcel Duchamp. Questioned in 1967 about the inspiration for his famous *Nude Descending a Staircase*, Duchamp replied that he saw Marey's chronophotography 'in the illustration of a book of Marey, where he showed men who were fencing, or horses in gallop with a system of dotted lines delineating the different movements. That is how he explained the idea of an elementary parallelism. It is a bit pretentious and formulaic, but amusing. That is what gave me the idea for the execution of the nude descending a staircase.'[13]

The staircase is a recurring theme in many of these stories. Coulomb's observation of a young man climbing a staircase hewn out of the rock face of a

Marcel Duchamp's *Nude Descending a Staircase.*

[11] Rabinbach, p. 97.
[12] *Ibid.*, p. 103.
[13] Quoted in *Ibid.*, p. 115.

mountain, or the servant running up stairs only to jump on a lift to force it down and thereby raise water, Muybridge's photographs of a man walking up stairs and Duchamp's nude descending the staircase, all represent the sequencing of time and motion by one of the oldest technologies available: the staircase. By varying the ratio between the treads and the risers (horizontal and vertical progress), one can ascend or descend quickly with great effort, or slowly with minimum effort. And beyond this use of the staircase as a mechanical lever lies the fertile field of staircase as metaphor, pressed into service from the Biblical Genesis to the Hollywood films of Busby Berkeley.

Ever since Jacob dreamed of 'a ladder set up on the earth, and the top of it reached to heaven: and behold the angels of God ascending and descending on it', stairways have been a powerful symbol of ascent (good event) and descent (bad). All good things, like success, redemption, happiness and eternal bliss, lie at the top of the steps and their opposites at the bottom. Rulers spiritual and secular appear at the top, while supplicants and subjects huddle at the foot. The stairway to Paradise traditionally is the most important. Today, however, the step-by-step process of a spaceshuttle launch, dramatically marked by the spoken sequence, '5–4–3–2–1-We have liftoff!' comes as close as possible to sending people into the heavens. In the Great Chain of Being, many at the bottom labour so that a few at the top may prosper, and everyone in between has a proper place.

Today, besides the space shuttle for the few, we have The Twelve Steps for the many. Originated by Alcoholics Anonymous, Step 1 admits powerlessness over alcohol, or some other chemical or behavioural problem, Step 2 expresses belief and faith in a 'Power greater than ourselves', and so by stages on to Step 12 in which, after a 'spiritual awakening', the redeemed reach out to others in need. According to one enthusiast, 'the rewards of working the Steps can be great' because 'the healing comes from that place deep within each of us that connects us to our Higher Power'.[14] It has been estimated that today some 15 million Americans take part in such 'recovery' groups.[15]

There are other ways of getting up to heaven. One can be 'saved' in an instant, or 'raptured up' in the last moments, both of which presume an instantaneous transport from below to above, saving the hard work of climbing the steps one by one. It is the genius of stairs that they create a sequence, bridging a

[14] Veronica Ray, *Design for Growth: Twelve Steps for Adult Children* (San Francisco: Harper & Row, 1989), pp. 106, 1.
[15] Wendy Kaminer, *I'm Dysfunctional, You're Dysfunctional: The Recovery Movement and Other Self-Help Fashions* (New York: Vintage Books, 1993), p. 80.

■ And he dreamed, and behold a ladder set up on the earth, and the top of it reached to heaven: and behold the angels of God ascending and descending on it.

GENESIS, *28:12*

gap in manageable steps, so that everyone who chooses may ascend to the heights. In this way, says Jonathan Miller, the staircase is like 'an engine, in which the moving parts happen to be the person who uses it'.[16]

The staircase entered the vocabulary of architecture in prehistoric times; the exterior of ancient temples of Mexico and Central America are simply great, theatrical staircases leading up to a sacred (often sacrificial) area at the top. In the West this use of steps reached its zenith in the grand staircases of Baroque palaces and public buildings, no coincidence in the era of powerful monarchs. In the architecture of the nineteenth century and continuing up to our own buildings – from libraries to hospitals, concert halls to schools – the public is met by an imposing flight of steps up which one must proceed to accomplish one's purpose. All technologies have cultural meanings that transcend the practical, but few demonstrate these so obviously as the staircase.

The logic and the irony of steps to redemption are demonstrated in the history of the prison wheel, introduced into Great Britain as a 'hard labour' alternative to execution and transportation for criminals. Developed in 1818 by William (later Sir William) Cubitt, it had precedents aplenty, ranging from Asian foot pumps

[16] Jonathan Miller, 'Introduction' to *Steps and Stairs*.

from the second century A.D. to the great lifting wheels shown in Breughel paintings. Cubitt's machine looked like a very wide waterwheel, upon the paddles of which a row of convicts climbed endlessly in the same spot, turning the wheel and its axle. The wheel of punishment also had some form of machinery, used either for productive work like milling grain or merely to dissipate the energies of the unfortunate workers. By 1842 it was claimed that 109 of the kingdom's 200 jails and houses of correction used the Cubitt wheel.

This Sisyphean labour was meant both to punish and redeem the prisoners, and in 1895 Oscar Wilde became perhaps its most famous victim. This sort of punishment, by such a theatrical and ritualized device, nicely epitomized, as its historian David H. Shayt has noted, 'the segmentation of time, space, and behavior in [Michel] Foucault's diabolical view of punishment (and public life)'.[17] As a fundamentally labour *wasting* machine, the prison treadmill shares an ironic kinship with the contemporary exercise staircases (or step machines) of the more fortunate today.

The treadmill erected at Brixton Prison in London, installed to improve discipline.

[17] David H. Shayt, 'Stairway to Redemption: America's Encounter with the British Prison Treadmill', *Technology and Culture*, 30 (October, 1989), 934.

Here too, self-improvement – indeed a kind of redemption – is only some steps away. Stairmaster, a leading brand, is equipped with 'resistance controls and a computerized, ergometric monitor that displays the user's climbing speed in steps per minute, caloric loss, power output in watts, heart rate, and total work performed in kilogramme-metres. An electronic beep sounds at the completion of each flight (sixteen steps)'. And this stairway too is spectacle. The ranks of near-perfect bodies, clothed in Lycra and working out like Muybridge's models, is no little part of the attraction.

It will be no surprise by now that, with industrialization, came marked alternatives to the stairs. In order to take advantage of new building techniques that allowed for buildings over five or six stories, the lift was borrowed from industry and used to raise people to new and literally dizzying heights. In 1852 Elisha Otis made some safety improvements in an industrial lift with which he was working; he took out patents for the device, and nine years before his early death began a career as a manufacturer. His improvement was to place racks on the inside surface of the vertical posts between which the lift worked. On the bottom of the cage itself pawls were attached in such a way that when the car stopped, or should the lifting mechanism fail, they would engage the rack and prevent the cage falling. The Otis elevator became the world standard, moving people smoothly and quickly up and down in department stores, apartment buildings, the new skyscrapers, and such monuments as the Eiffel Tower.

The staircase itself was modernized by the turn of the century with the introduction of the escalator, from its earliest times closely associated with spectacle and entertainment. In 1896, Jesse Wilford Reno introduced his 'inclined elevator' (patented 1892) at Coney Island, the great amusement park and pleasure garden on the edge of New York City. Within two years he was installing them in large department stores and at the 1900 Paris Universal Exposition his was one of four designs for a similar purpose. In 1911 he was bought out by the Otis elevator company.

One of Reno's rivals, the American Charles Seeberger, had already bought up several competing patents and persuaded the Otis company to build machines based upon them. It was he who trademarked the invented word Escalator, thus spawning the terms escalate and escalation. His moving stairways were elegant,

with their oak slats and leather-muffled wheels and his 1900 Paris Exposition installation yielded nothing to the theatrical stairways of architects. His most daring machine was one installed in the London Underground in 1906. It curved upward in a spiral, slanting to one side as it rose. Its complicated design proved fatal to its success, however, and it was soon abandoned.

The escalator as spectacle, suggested by Reno's 1896 Coney Island installation, was raised to a theory by critics of the 1939 New York World's Fair. It was realized that contemporary visitors, unlike their Victorian counterparts, were more interested in process than products, and exhibitors like the General Motors Corporation in their display of 'the world of tomorrow', gave visitors just that. An article, 'Drama and Crowds – Direct Sources of and Materials for Design', which appeared in the *Architectural Record*, claimed that 'the greatest discovery in New York was the discovery of the crowd both as actor and as decoration of great power. The designers found out that the crowd's greatest pleasure is in the crowd.'[18]

The apotheosis of the crowd-as-spectacle appears in the giant shopping malls which dot America and Canada, and are now invading Britain. As Margaret Crawford notes, 'the enclosed mall compressed and intensified space. Glass-enclosed elevators and zigzagging escalators added dynamic vertical and diagonal movement to the basic horizontal plan of the mall.'[19] The 'people mover' or moving sidewalk, a mechanical cousin of the escalator most often now found in major airports, was first used at Chicago's Columbia Exposition in 1893, then appeared in Harrod's department store in 1898, and finally made it to the London Underground (connecting the London Transport circulating area at Waterloo train station with the platforms of the Waterloo and City London Underground line) in 1960. Its most spectacular, and post-modern, application however, must certainly be that in the underground connection between United Airline terminals 'B' and 'C' at O'Hare airport in Chicago. As passengers move towards each end of the tunnel (and towards each other) they are accompanied by a rainbow of neon lights suspended from a mirrored ceiling and lighting up sequentially at a pace somewhat faster than the passengers. At the same time an electronic and somewhat 'New Age' form of music surrounds the traveller, resolving gradually as the journey ends into the courteous instruction: 'The moving walkway is now ending, please look down.'

The moving walkway of technological change is not coming to an end,

An 1877 engraving of an hydraulic elevator with a jigger mechanism which was worked by a rope passing through the car.

[18] Quoted in Warren I. Susman, *Culture as History: The Transformation of American Society in the Twentieth Century* (New York: Pantheon Books, 1984), p. 218.

[19] Margaret Crawford, 'The World in a Shopping Mall', *Variations of a Theme Park: The New American City and the End of Public Space*, ed. Michael Sorkin (New York: Noonday Press, 1992), p. 22.

however. Just as the digital clock has largely displaced the analogue clock (spring driven, with hands sweeping across a face), so digital (discrete) is replacing analogue (continuous) in imaging, including photography. In the old photographs, closer inspection revealed greater detail but at a loss of clarity and focus. Now, as William Mitchell explains in *The Reconfigured Eye: Visual Truth in the Post-Photographic Era*, 'images are encoded digitally by uniformly subdividing the picture plane into a finite Cartesian grid of cells (known as *pixels*) and specifying the intensity or color of each cell by means of an integer number drawn from some limited range'.[20]

The analogue photograph cannot be copied without a loss of quality, as one sees even with copies of xerox copies. A digital copy, however, is in no respect different from its original. Moreover, not only does one not know whether one has an 'original' (whatever that now means), one cannot be sure that it is even a representation of reality. Computer manipulation of digital images does not simply 'change' pictures, it creates new ones. Again as Mitchell notes, 'digital imagers give meaning and value to computational readymades by appropriation, transformation, reprocessing, and recombination; we have', he concludes, 'entered the age of electrobricolage.'[21] Like the crowds at malls, process is gaining the advantage over product.

Finally, however, it is still the product that matters, whether through the appropriation of spectacle to promote consumerism or the use of 'electrobricolage' to replace our reality with someone else's. New frontiers of digital manipulation, including teleportation, are already being imagined. The American science writer Daniel S. Greenberg has, only half humorously, raised the alarm on this least credible of science fiction fantasies. He quotes the journal *Nature* as explaining that 'a physical object is equivalent to the information needed to construct it; the object can therefore be transported by transmitting the information along any conventional channel of telecommunications, the receiver using the information to reconstruct the object'.[22] Teleportation is perhaps the appropriate consequence of the segmenting and sequencing that has been such an integral part of modern life. The fantasy of instantaneous travel undercuts any remaining vestige of space and time as eternal verities which flow but never stop, pass but never end.

Left: an 1894 engraving of the electrically powered escalator at the Pennsylvania Railroad Company's Cortland Street Station in New York. **Right:** the escalator at O'Hare airport, Chicago.

[20] (Cambridge: MIT Press, 1992), p. 5.
[21] *Ibid.*, p. 7.
[22] Daniel S. Greenberg, 'Hey, Scotty, don't beam us up', (Cleveland) *Plain Dealer*, 28 April 1993.

Chapter four

MAKES NO SENSE

■ *'All my means are sane, my motive and my object mad.'*

CAPT. AHAB IN *Moby Dick* BY HERMAN MELVILLE[1]

William Heath Robinson's comic fantasy of the mass production of whitebait from his book *Inventions.*

[1] Quoted in Leo Marx, *The Machine in the Garden: Technology and the Pastoral Ideal in America* (New York: Oxford Univ. Press, 1964), p. 318.

N THE UNITED STATES and, at last count, thirty-one other countries around the world, McDonald's fries are uniformly appealing in appearance and delicious in taste. Teenagers need only fifteen minutes of training to make this perfect product and hit their peak work efficiency with half an hour's experience. The combination of a computer-controlled temperature probe in the hot oil, and a special scoop that measures exact amounts for each serving, make every order the same – and the young workers equally interchangeable. The labour turnover at McDonald's is high, but when a worker can be trained in fifteen minutes it hardly matters if she or he quits at the end of their first day. As one observer has noted, 'It's job organization, not malice, that allows (almost requires) McDonald's workers to be handled like paper plates. They feel disposable because they are.'[2] It is a long way from Henry Ford's River Rouge plant in Michigan to a McDonald's in Moscow, but the path is straight and narrow.

In 1926 a ghost-written entry on mass production appeared in Henry Ford's name in the thirteenth edition of the *Encyclopaedia Britannica*. Mass production, it insisted, 'is the focusing upon a manufacturing project of the principles of power, accuracy, economy, system, continuity, speed, and repetition'.[3] Contemplated individually, these words speak mostly of virtue, of what is necessary for science, progress, and modernism. As a collective imperative, however, they chill the heart. During the 1960s there were those who condemned the 'insane rationality' of the American Pentagon for planning scenarios of thermonuclear holocaust, and there was something of the same idiot *savant* about Henry Ford and Frederick Winslow Taylor, the midwives of the twentieth century. The passionate urge to rationalize, the better to control; to control in order to dominate; and to dominate in order to stave off the terror of encountering difference, all this harnessed reason to, if not madness, at least a profound degree of irrationality. Nowhere was this better seen than in the automobile industry of the early twentieth century.

When the Honourable Evelyn Henry Ellis, M.P., decided to buy a car in 1894, he went to Paris to negotiate its construction with the firm Panhard et Levassor. A scant seven years before, Emile Levassor had met Gottlieb Daimler, founder of the firm that still makes the Mercedes-Benz, and acquired the right to

[2] Barbara Garson, *The Electronic Sweatshop* (New York, 1988), p. 37.
[3] *Encyclopaedia Britannica*, 13th ed.

make his gasoline engines. Panhard et Levassor mainly made metal-cutting saws, but by 1894 several hundred automobiles a year as well, using the *Système Panhard* with rear-wheel drive, engine in front, and passengers between the two.

The car Ellis bought was, for all intents and purposes, unique. The Panhard et Levassor workers were skilled craftspeople, some of whom were independent artisans working by the job in the P&L shops, and some even worked in their own shops in other parts of the city. Ellis described the car he wanted, including engine controls, brake and transmission on the left rather than the right side (the steering tiller remained in the middle). The hundreds of individual parts were made in different shops all over Paris by artisans using different gauges so that in the end

Preparing food in the kitchen of a McDonald's restaurant. It takes only fifteen minutes to train a new employee.

no two would quite fit together. Final assembly at P&L began with workers filing two parts so that they would fit, then a third to match up with them, and so on until the car was assembled. As a result of 'dimensional creep', the finished car differed significantly from its original plans. Ease of repair was not a significant problem for Ellis, however, since like all wealthy motorists, he employed a professional chauffeur/mechanic to assist him with the machine.

Once test drives revealed the automobile to be to his satisfaction, Ellis returned to Britain and drove triumphantly from Southampton to his country seat, taking only five hours and thirty-two minutes (excluding stops) to cover the fifty-six miles and becoming the first person to drive an automobile in the country. He averaged nearly ten miles an hour on the road, well over the legal British highway limit of four miles per hour, but he soon supported a successful parliamentary effort to repeal the notorious Red Flag law which had been passed in

Right: Henry Ford in his first car.
Above: Ford's River Rouge plant in Michigan in America.

4 This story is taken from James P. Womack *et al.*, *The Machine That Changed the World* (New York: Rawson Associates, 1990), pp. 21–24.

1865 at the behest of stagecoach operators to kill off a growing commercial traffic in steam-powered omnibuses. Fourteen miles per hour now became the legal limit for highway speed.[4]

Evelyn Ellis's automobile, preserved today in the Science Museum in London, was a superb example of the craft tradition of manufacture which prevailed in all industrial areas of the world at the turn of the century. Within a decade, however, Henry Ford of Dearborn, Michigan, was initiating that series of industrial innovations that would revolutionize all manner of manufacture, beginning with automobiles.

Ford built his first car in 1896. He was by no means unique; by then more than 500 American patents had been taken out for motor vehicles and two major periodicals had appeared to meet the need of enthusiasts. Like dozens of other hopeful builders he established a firm, the Ford Motor Company, in 1903 and by 1907 he had effective control of the management of the operation. In 1908, he introduced his classic Model-T, a light, flexible, efficient and cheap design which became the first 'car for the masses'.

From the beginning, Ford was able to build upon a strong American manufacturing tradition. This included the standardization of parts (called 'armoury practice' after its origins in the government small-arms factories early in the nineteenth century), a flow process which produced in a continuous stream rather than in batches, and evolving notions of work efficiencies, soon to culminate in Frederick Winslow Taylor's system of Scientific Management. In its first year, the Ford Company turned out one car for every twelve workers. This ratio of productivity was not achieved in Europe for many years, and not at the Morris Motors works in Britain until 1934.[5]

Not content with this initial level of productivity, and wishing to bring down his prices in order to tap a mass automobile market in America, Ford hired and turned loose in his shop a group of young engineers and technicians who transformed his entire operation. A single standard of gauges was established so that all parts could be made to the same specification. Metal-stamping techniques and electric-resistance welding were introduced from the bicycle industry, one in which many automobile manufacturers in France, Britain and America had direct experience. Machine tools were clustered around the parts to be made rather than grouped by type. Finally, in a fine piece of lateral thinking, the example of the great Midwestern slaughter house (in a sense, large disassembly lines) was borrowed and reversed so that cars were put together as they went along, as the unfortunate animals had been taken apart as they hung on a moving and endless chain in front of workers. In 1913–14, first for sub-assemblies and then for putting together the car itself, Ford's new assembly lines made extraordinary gains in efficiency for a remarkably small monetary investment. Between October and December 1913, the first assembly line for chassis reduced the time required to put a car together from twelve-and-a-half hours to two hours and forty minutes. Model-T production jumped from 13 840 in 1909 to 585 388 in 1916; at the same time its price dropped from $950 to $360.

The assembly line innovations took place at Ford's huge Highland Park plant which opened in 1910. The modernist architect Albert Kahn, a favourite of automobile moguls, designed a four storey building, 865 ft × 75 ft, with 50 000 sq ft of glass. Other buildings joined it along a line, one 860 ft × 57 ft and yet another, 840 ft × 140 ft. This giant plant was dwarfed in 1916 when work began

Frederick Winslow Taylor.

[5] James J. Flink, *The Automobile Age* (Cambridge: MIT Press, 1988), p. 43.

on Ford's enormous River Rouge plant, the site of what historian James J. Flink has called 'intensified Fordism'.[6] A 2000-acre plot of land near Detroit was turned into what must surely have been the single largest and most integrated production plant in existence.

The world's largest foundry was erected, 595 ft × 1188 ft, and within a few years 10 000 workers made castings there for Ford cars and tractors. Other buildings were constructed, and a 30 000 kilowatt power plant was brought on line. Dredging created a port; a railway system was purchased, and Ford vertically integrated his operations so that by the end of the 1920s the Ford Company had iron mines, lumber mills, coal mines, glass plants and a rubber plantation in Brazil, all to produce the raw materials needed to feed the productive colossus at the Rouge and Highland Park. The railway and a fleet of ships connected the two.

But in the handling of workers, that most recalcitrant and unpredictable of the factors of production, Ford was less successful. Fordism, as it was universally called, not only created a great, integrated machine for turning out cars, but pioneered a workforce as standardized and interchangeable as his automobiles and as dedicated to a single purpose as the thousands of machine tools that they tended. For his very first innovations, Ford began shifting skill from workers to their machines, and decision-making to management. Thus were artisans reduced to machine tenders and, more significantly, unskilled and semi-skilled workers trapped in a productive process which allowed no opportunity for advancement through the mastering of new skills and tasks. The division of labour, at least as old as Adam Smith, was carried to an extreme and the pace of work was dictated by the movement of the line. Not until Charlie Chaplin's masterpiece *Modern Times* appeared in the 1930s was life on the line captured for the average person, but once seen, the image of the little tramp literally caught in the relentless cogs of the factory made a memorable impression. The industrial proletariat did not first emerge in Detroit, but under the conditions of Fordism their fate became synonymous with alienation and exploitation.

With the destruction of an older style of work discipline, one based on skill, apprenticeship, stints set by labour and other forms of the shop-floor power exerted by workers, a new discipline had to be devised. This, too, the Ford managers made up as they went along, even as they had built up their technical

[6] *Ibid.*, p. 49.

innovations. The 'human element of production', as it was called, included pre-industrial habits and expectations on the part of recent emigrant workers, absenteeism, tardiness, soldiering (slacking off), union activities, and an astonishing rate of labour turnover. In 1913 ten per cent of the workforce at Highland Park was absent each day, and that same year there was a staggering turnover of 370 per cent of the labour force.

Ford's first response was to institute a menu of paternalistic measures which were finding a place in other industries. A savings and loan bank was organized to help workers save for hard times, a 'job ladder' was instituted to try to reinstate job mobility. Other steps were taken to win worker loyalty to the firm. In January 1914, Ford instituted his famous Five Dollar Day, effectively giving a substantial raise in pay to all those workers who agreed to improve themselves and their lifestyles in certain ways approved of by the company. To implement this a Sociology Department was established. Besides such useful steps as organizing English classes for immigrants, however, the department also made bold to visit workers' homes, make enquiries about intimate details of their lives, and in general invade workers' privacy.

After the First World War this paternalism was abandoned in favour of a more harsh and repressive policy of labour spies and violence. Harry Bennett, a former prize fighter with underworld crime connections, led a gang of thugs and labour spies called the Service Department which was known to intimidate and, when 'necessary', physically assault workers. In 1928 the pro-business *New York Times* called Ford 'an industrial fascist – the Mussolini of Detroit'.[7]

The crude repression of worker resistance at Ford was not the worst of it, of course. By 1911, the classic manifesto *The Principles of Scientific Management*, Frederick Winslow Taylor's utopian dream of a science-based labour efficiency had been published and was being widely discussed. Taylor had been born in Germantown, Pennsylvania, in 1856 of prosperous and privileged parents. But before he had the chance to enter Harvard University, as his family had planned, he developed weak eyesight and instead went to work in the machine shops of the Enterprise Hydraulic Works in Philadelphia. He enrolled to matriculate in mechanical engineering at the Stevens Institute of Technology and in 1884 became chief engineer of the Midvale Steel Works. A few years later he set up as a

---

[7] *Ibid.*, p. 125.

Charlie Chaplin in *Modern Times* which portrayed life on the factory line.

consulting engineer, with 'Systematizing Shop Management and Manufacturing Costs a Speciality'. Taylor's developing concepts of shop management were put to the test in 1898 when he was hired by the Bethlehem Steel Company to systematize their operations.

By 1911 when he published his book, Taylor wanted to point out 'the great loss which the whole country is suffering through inefficiency in almost all of our daily acts'. Secondly, he wanted to 'try to convince the reader that the remedy for this inefficiency lies in systematic management, rather than in searching for some unusual or extraordinary man'. And finally, he sought to 'prove that the best management is a true science, resting upon clearly defined laws, rules, and principles, as a foundation. And further to show that the fundamental principles of scientific management are applicable to all kinds of human activities, from our simplest individual acts to the work of our great corporations.'

Taylor constructed his system in equal part from shop work as he had seen and experienced it and his own class prejudices. Echoing the cry of mill owners from the earliest days of the Industrial Revolution, Taylor insisted that 'scientific management ... [has] for its very foundation the firm conviction that the true interests of [management and labour] ... are one and the same. ...' The 'greatest prosperity', he continued, 'can exist only as a result of the greatest possible productivity of the men and machines of establishment – that is, when each man and each machine are turning out the largest possible output'.

This simple truth, as he saw it, was obscured by three common sets of circumstances. First, the approach of workers everywhere to their jobs is neither to be overworked nor work themselves out of a job. Second, management every-where tries to squeeze ever more work out of labour, recognizing no practical limit to toil. And the third is, 'the inefficient rule-of-thumb methods [that is, those derived from practice], which are still almost universal in all trades, and in practising which our workmen waste a large part of their effort'. It was central to his faith that 'among all the various methods and implements used in each element of each trade there is always one method and one implement which is quicker and better than any of the rest. These can only be discovered or developed through a scientific study and analysis of all of the methods and implements in use, together with accurate, minute, motion and time study. This involves', he insists, 'the gradual substitution of science for rule of thumb throughout the mechanic arts. ...'

This implied the wholesale transfer of skill and responsibility to management. Shopfloor control of work, based on hard-won skills and the enforcement of traditional stints (the amount of work to be accomplished in a given period), was to be eliminated. Efficiency engineers with stopwatches discovered how the work process was currently carried out, the process was 'scientifically' reorganized to maximize efficiency, then the new tasks, tools, and work rates were given back to the workers in the form of instructions issued from planning departments. In Taylor's words, 'the managers assume ... the burden of gathering together all of the traditional knowledge which in the past has been possessed by the workmen and then of classifying, tabulating, and reducing this knowledge to rules, laws, and formulae which are immensely helpful to the workmen in doing their daily work'. Taylor was a violent foe of welfare schemes, such as those instituted in the Ford plants, but he did insist that workers should be allowed to share in the gains in productivity which his plan would presumably provide. There was, however, no way of forcing management to share its windfall, especially since it was likely to last only until competitors also adopted the scheme.

The actual number of shops that installed Taylorism in its entirety is not recorded. It is not even clear whether or not Henry Ford tried to use scientific management in this sense. Taylor himself, who held over one hundred patents and was elected President of the American Society of Mechanical Engineers, looked beyond machine shops and automobile factories and insisted that his scientific management was applicable to any activity that was being carried on inefficiently (as, he believed, all were). The concept of 'efficiency' became a craze in the United States in the years around the Great War, invoked to justify every reform from teaching immigrants English to sterilizing socially defective peoples in the name of eugenics and social efficiency. Intelligence tests were applied to the American Expeditionary Force to try to put the right soldier in the right job, a prohibition on alcohol was promoted as a way to use grain supplies more efficiently and create a more efficient (that is sober) workforce.

Terrified, as many of his class, by what was believed to be a rising tide of industrial violence in the United States as well as in the rest of the world, Taylor sought to draw the veil of 'science' over the naked advantage of management. Addressing the United States Congress in 1912, Taylor explained 'the great revolution that takes place in the mental attitude of the two parties under scientific management in that both sides take their eyes off of the division of the surplus as the all-important matter, and together turn their attention toward increasing the size of the surplus until this surplus becomes so large that it is unnecessary to quarrel over how it shall be divided.'[8] The temptation to use technology in order to avoid facing questions of social justice was as old as the American republic and, perhaps, not entirely limited to that country alone.

Another efficiency engineer, a great admirer of Taylor but not acknowledged as a disciple by the latter, was Frank Gilbreth (1868–1924). A former brick-layer and building contractor, Gilbreth pioneered in the filming of work processes. He could then analyze the film frame by frame, breaking each activity down into its constituent movements: the reach, the grasp, etc. He called these 'therbligs' – Gilbreth (almost) spelt backwards. Gilbreth's wife Lillian was the mother of their twelve children (the novel *Cheaper by the Dozen* was the story of their family), earned a doctorate in psychology, and worked with her husband in their consulting engineering practice.

After Frank Gilbreth's untimely death, Lillian attempted to carry on their work but met with the solid distrust of a patriarchal business and engineering world. Her eventual success lay in concentrating on the home 'efficiency movement' which sought to apply Taylorism to the domestic workplace. Advocating what she called the Gilbreth Motion Study Kitchen or, more commonly, the Kitchen Efficient, she sought to liberate women from the drudgeries of housework not by removing them from the home, nor by dividing the work equitably with their husbands, but by showing the housewife how to do her work more efficiently and 'intelligently'. Observers were already noticing that innumerable housewives were suffering from something very close to clinical depression, brought on by not only the hard and endless cycle of housework but also by the rigid gender structure that dictated that such work was all her responsibility. By working efficiently, some reformers hoped, the symptoms could be removed without removing the root cause of the malady. The Kitchen Efficient would be a boon to the housewife because:

[8] 'Taylor's Testimony Before the Special House Committee', *Scientific Management* (New York: Harper & Brothers, 1947), pp. 29–30.

Here I may be a Scientist
Who measures as she makes.
Here I may be an Artist
Creating as she bakes.
Here busy heart and brain and hand
May think and feel and do.
A kitchen is a happy place
To make a dream come true.[9]

If the vision of the happy (because efficient) housewife sounded wildly at odds with the increasing alienation of factory labour, it was because the industrialization in the home had exactly the opposite effect to that at River Rouge. As electrical appliances created more efficient work processes, as servants began to disappear and as housework became less specialized rather than more, the middle-class housewife was downgraded from management to labourer. Far from losing its meaning, housework became profoundly symbolic of a wife and mother's love for her family and a measure of her fundamental character.

In 1935 Lillian Gilbreth carried her message to Britain for the Sixth International Congress for Scientific Management, Domestic Section in London. Delegates attended a session on 'Food planning in the Home to ensure satisfactory nutrition with a minimum expenditure of time, money and labour', presided over by the dowager Lady Nunburnholme; another was a description of 'Palestine with its primitive orientals using time-honoured implements not noticeably different from those mentioned in the Old Testament'. They also heard Gilbreth's quite sensible presentation. She was reported to have said that, 'in a world growing more and more scientific, the housewife's point of view must remain the ultimate one, [and] emphasized that the ideal development must be a happy collaboration of theory, scientific testing and household practice'.[10]

Lillian Gilbreth was neither the first nor the only conduit by which American ideas of efficiency found their way to Europe. For one thing, a steady stream of visitors appeared at Highland Park and River Rouge to see first-hand the miracle of modernism. Making this pilgrimage were André Citroën, Louis Renault, Giovanni Agnelli of Fiat, William Morris and Herbert Austin from England, and a host of

[9] Quoted in Frank B. Gilbreth, Jr., *Time Out for Happiness* (New York: Thomas Y. Crowell Co., 1970), p. 212.
[10] Muriel Watson, 'Women Discuss House Planning and Home Management', *The Electrical Age*, 2 (October, 1935), 941.

*S*ometimes the office is no different to the assembly line as this 1988 cartoon from *Punch* shows.

Russians. The ideas flowed most directly and perhaps with greatest impact through the Ford company's many plants in Britain and on the Continent. By the time of the Great War, Ford was the largest automobile manufacturer in Britain, turning out some 50 000 Model-T cars, trucks, and ambulances between 1914 and 1918. Between October 1919 and December 1920, British Ford sold 46 000 vehicles. Ford never had the same success on the Continent as in Britain where, in 1929, ground was broken at Dagenham for a new plant designed to turn out 120 000 units a year.

Not surprisingly, such numbers were achieved by using Fordist methods. In 1914, Ford's Trafford Park plant already turned out 12 500 cars a year with only 1 500 workers. The next year the dedicated machine tools and moving assembly line were installed, along with other new features from Highland Park. Even so, the adoption of Fordism was patchy. Sunbeam played with a moving assembly line as early as 1913, but with sales of only 2 000 units a year it hardly seemed worthwhile. Fiat, in Italy, tried the same innovation in its Turin plant that same year, but its wide range of products made the necessary standardization difficult. Not until 1936, when it built a huge plant at Mirafiori to build its little Topolino model, did Fiat finally commit itself to Ford methods. In retrospect it is clear that two major problems intervened outside the United States. The first was the absence of any commitment on the part of management to making and selling a great number of cheap, standardized cars. The second was the understandable opposition of organized labour to any attempt to discipline them with Fordist and Taylorite work processes.

The massive strike at Longbridge in 1929, when Austin tried to install a continuous-flow assembly line and reclassify job skills, could have been predicted. Whereas American automobile plants were largely unorganized, Ford discovered a strong craft union tradition in Britain. Even after the organization of the United Auto Workers in America, manufacturers had to deal with only this one industrial union. In Britain, in contrast, twenty-two different craft unions controlled different parts of the labour process. Capitalists, too, seemed unready for Fordism. By 1914 advocates of English distinctiveness deeply distrusted what appeared to be an American willingness to put greed and a lust for power before any more humane values. Managers, it appeared, were reluctant to degrade their workers in this peculiarly American style. 'Most of us English', wrote J.B. Priestley some years later, 'still cherish an instinctive feeling that men come first and that machines should come a long way afterwards.'[11]

If the miracles of modern American mass production fit badly with British habits and prejudices, they found a ready audience on the Continent. In France, some aspects of Taylorism were taken up early – in 1909 at the Renault plant and the next year at Panhard et Levasser. In important ways, however, the *idea* of Taylorism had a greater impact than any particular industrial application. By the 1920s it was seen not only as a characteristic feature of American life, but as a possible way out from the dilemma of cultural failure represented by the Great War. Especially, as it turned out, for the European Right, Taylorism and Fordism suggested not just a method of labour relations, but an agenda for social policies.

The conditions of the Great War proved a fertile nursery for the young Taylorism. The clash of nation states demanded the subordination of class conflicts to national survival. Neither labour nor management needed to fear overproduction or price competition. Technical expertise put to the service of production benefited all classes as both wages and profits were guaranteed by the needs of the state. Moreover, the old powers of both unions and companies to limit output, resist new machines, and otherwise pursue narrow, parochial interests, could be swept

[11] Quoted in Martin J. Wiener, *English Culture and the Decline of the Industrial Spirit, 1850–1980* (Cambridge: Cambridge University Press, 1981), p. 88.

The assembly of the Model-T Ford (centre) at Highland Park circa 1914. Left (descending): flywheel production; bodies arriving; the petrol tank deck; fitting the starting device. Below: testing the chassis (left) and the body deck (right).

away in the name of disinterested expertise and national need. Social harmony and central authority produced not only vast amounts of munitions, but a cohesive body politic which would have seemed utopian only a few years before.

The price was paid in squandered lives and treasure, and in challenging the very superiority of liberal, bourgeois society. In England, the liberal regime remained firm and the middle-class relatively contented with the social order. On the Continent however, both Left and Right sought for some new basis of class relations. Even before the war Italian Futurists had been attracted to the machine as a symbol of speed, violence and death, and drew upon these for the basis of a new artistic movement. The 1909 Manifesto of F.T. Marinetti announced:

> ... We wish to glorify War – the only health giver of the world – militarism, patriotism, the destructive arm of the Anarchist, the beautiful Ideas that kill, the contempt for woman. ...

Right: Alfred Krupp and (above) the Krupp factory at Essen in Germany in 1912.

... We shall sing of the great crowds in the excitement of labour, pleasure and rebellion; of the multi-coloured and polyphonic surf of revolutions in modern capital cities; of the nocturnal vibration of arsenals and workshops beneath their violent electric moons; of the greedy stations swallowing smoking snakes; of factories suspended from the clouds by their strings of smoke; of bridges leaping like gymnasts over the diabolical cutlery of sunbathed rivers; of adventurous liners scenting the horizon; of broad-chested locomotives prancing on the rails, like huge steel horses bridled with long tubes; and of the gliding flight of aeroplanes, the sound of whose screw is like the flapping of flags and the applause of an enthusiastic crowd.[12]

Mussolini was much taken with the Futurists. As the Nazis gained strength in Germany during the 1920s, they too turned to what one historian has called a position of 'Reactionary Modernism'. The Enlightenment was rejected as Jewish and, therefore, internationalist in nature. In the ideas of Taylor and Ford, and the whole machine culture epitomized by America, they discovered a deep vein of irrationality, of romanticism, which allowed them to grasp notions of efficiency and the conquest of nature while at the same time drawing strength and inspiration from the 'blood and soil' of the German heartland.

In Fritz Lang's masterpiece of German Expressionism, *Metropolis* (a film which allegedly much attracted Hitler), the master of the city had created a society in which the masters lived a sybaritic life among the offices and pleasure gardens of the upper level, the machinery to keep the city alive worked at a level below ground, and beneath that lived the workers. This labour force, virtually a part of the machinery, is bestial and ignorant, degraded by the mechanized work. The master's dream is to replace them with robots, and for these he turns not to scientists but to an inventor/magician, already made somewhat less than human through the loss of a hand during his experiments. The rustic cottage in which the inventor lives and works stands in the middle of, but in striking contrast to, the gleaming, modern 'metropolis' of skyscrapers and autogiros, a stage set which became the standard for all futuristic cities since. The cottage in the city is a powerful symbol of the older, more organic, pre-modern springs of technological

[12] Quoted in Joshua C. Taylor,
Futurism (New York: Museum of
Modern Art, New York 1961),
p. 124.

creation. It bears a striking resemblance to the old home of the Krupp family which was piously, but incongruously, preserved for posterity in the middle of their vast steel works. The Lang film and the Krupp's filial piety echoed the already obvious Nazi commitment to efficiency and romanticism and epitomized the kernel of irrationality at the heart of Ford and Taylor's miracle. In the gas ovens of the Holocaust, the mass production lines of Highland Park returned to their roots in the disassembly lines of earlier abattoirs.

In the Soviet Union Lenin, too, embraced Taylorism. The rush to industrialize a largely peasant society, and without the aid of a trained bourgeoisie, led to the hopeful embracing of any formula that promised to bring order out of chaos. The widely publicized image of wholesome young men and women from collective farms embracing tractors was only a striking example of a much larger and more fundamental desire to harness Taylorism and Fordism to socialism. It is not surprising that after Stalin's purge of the older cadre of engineers, and the education of a new generation of the sons and daughters of workers and peasants to replace them, the Soviet Union became probably the first nation to be ruled by a committee of engineers.

The dream of social engineering led perhaps inevitably to a turn to technocracy, the rule by a technical elite. In the film *Things to Come* (based on H.G. Wells's *The Shape of Things to Come*), England is thrust into barbarism by a second world war. The country is eventually liberated by a cadre of scientists and engineers who had escaped the war and had managed to preserve 'civilization' in a distant place. With no appeal to democracy, but a firm dependence on truth and reason, the ruling body of technicians manages to maintain the peace, abolish poverty, conquer disease and build a gleaming nation of modern conveniences. Only then does ennui set in, to be overcome by the sending off of an attractive young couple to explore the universe.

Much of the attraction of Taylorism lay in its claim to political neutrality through the strict application of scientific laws. Henry L. Gantt, one of Taylor's most able disciples, put it most simply: 'What we need,' he wrote, 'is not more laws, but more facts, and the whole question will solve itself.'[13] While Taylorism was seen as primarily a way of disciplining and rationalizing labour, Fordism addressed the entire production process. As something of a counter measure,

[13] Quoted in Charles S. Maier, 'Between Taylorism and Technocracy: European ideologies and the vision of industrial productivity in the 1920s', *Journal of Contemporary History*, 5 (1970), 31.

Fordism gave room to the creative play of the entrepreneur, as against the disinterested expert proposed by Taylorism.

Both concepts were explored in the 1923 Czech play *R.U.R.*, by the brothers Capek, first produced that year at St Martin's Theatre. Apart from introducing the word 'robot' into the English language, the play relentlessly pursued the logic of Fordism. Rossum's Universal Robots were mass produced on a remote island (the theme speaks of isolation and self-containment, as a River Rouge) and sold round the world for factory work and, eventually, as soldiers. When the head of the works asks a visitor: 'What sort of worker do you think is the best from a practical point of view?' the visitor answers, 'The best? Perhaps the one who is most honest and hard-working.' 'No,' comes the reply, 'the cheapest. The one whose needs are the smallest. Young Rossum invented a worker with the minimum amount of requirements. He had to simplify him. He rejected everything that did not contribute directly to the progress of work.'[14] The dream of the manager was to put an end to human beings as labour. As robots produced goods at a cheaper and cheaper rate, 'everybody will be free from worry, and liberated from the degradation of labour. Everybody will live only to perfect himself'.[15]

In *R.U.R.*, as workers throughout Europe were replaced by robots, they rose only to be shot down by robot soldiers. At last, through circumstances and the further improvement of the machines, the robots themselves developed a sense of grievance, turned against their makers and killed the entire human race, a group which had already, significantly, stopped breeding. In the shadow of the Bolshevik revolution and the Great War, the story can be read as a cautionary tale against the mindless, insane pursuit of endless mechanization. Or it can be read as a warning against the attempt to reduce labour to the status of dumb beast with the 'minimum amount of requirements'. Either way, the dreams of Ford and Taylor were deeply implicated in such situations.

However, both Fordism and Taylorism in their extreme applications were already in retreat by the end of the 1920s. Henry Ford had tried to maintain his autonomy by building the vertically integrated company that was symbolized by the giant River Rouge plant, and by buying out his partners so that he alone controlled his empire. In his factories he savagely simplified his operations and produced a single model of automobile, the famous T. In the very year of *R.U.R.*,

[14] The Brothers Capek, *R.U.R.*
and The Insect Play (London:
Oxford University Press, 1961),
p. 9.
[15] *Ibid.*, p. 25.

General Motors, under the leadership of Alfred P. Sloan, initiated what he called the 'constant upgrading of product', better known today as planned obsolescence. The yearly model change, the nicely graded range of cars, from the lowly Chevrolet to the most expensive Cadillac, the setting up of the General Motors Acceptance Corporation (GMAC) to extend consumer credit to customers – all included under the new term of Sloanism – cut against the severe logic of Fordist standardization. General Motors integrated its production of parts and sub-assemblies, installed dedicated machine tools, adopted the moving assembly line, and turned out massive numbers of cars. Ford was forced to back away from his insistence on producing one model at the cheapest cost, and even had to design the Model A to try to compete with the Chevrolet. General Motors went on to become the world's largest corporation and helped make Detroit synonymous with mass production. It began to look as though the modern was here to stay.

But eras come and go. Though the idea of a post-modern age was propounded first in architecture, it found its way into industrial life as well. In 1950 a young Japanese engineer, Eiji Toyota, followed the path of many before him to the Ford River Rouge plant in Detroit. His family's automobile company, in operation for thirteen years, had managed to produce only 2685 cars. River Rouge turned out 7 000 every working day. Toyota studied the Rouge operation and returned to Japan with some ideas about how to borrow, and how to improve, the very model of mass production he had seen in America. Together with his production boss, Taiichi Ohno, he oversaw the creation of a new method of production later termed 'lean' by its American admirers.

Although lean production used many of the most important aspects of mass production, like the moving assembly line, it fundamentally rethought the entire process so that only half the floor space, half the tools, half the engineering time to produce changes, and half the workers were needed to produce the same number of cars. The major innovations included a commitment to quality control which not only allowed but required each worker 'on the line' to stop production when a defect appeared. Dedicated machine tools were replaced with reprogrammable general purpose models so that design changes in cars could be rapidly translated into production. Dealers sought the advice of customers and carried only a few models in their showrooms, most cars sold being manufactured to order. Con-

Robots welding car bodies on the assembly line of the Mazda car plant at Hiroshima in Japan.

tractors for sub-assemblies were brought into the design process and encouraged to co-operate rather than compete. Parts were delivered 'just in time' so that large inventories were dispensed with. In 1987 the comparison of a General Motors plant in the United States and a Toyota plant in Japan showed that cars in the latter were assembled in half the time (sixteen hours compared with thirty-one), with a third of the defects, and in half the occupied area.

The new efficiencies being achieved by Japanese automobile manufacturers, plus their ability to produce cars with lower fuel consumption and creating less pollution, have destroyed the myth of the superiority of mass production. Most centrally it has fatally undermined Detroit's role as mentor to the world in all things industrial. Now it is Ford, General Motors, and Chrysler that visit Japan searching for better ways to produce cars. Press reports in 1993 indicated that

Robots welding on the assembly line of the LeBaron car at the Chrysler plant in Missouri in America.

Toyota, Honda and Nissan were operating or building plants in Britain aimed at making upwards of three-quarters of a million cars a year, mainly for export to the Continent. One expert at the University of Wales said 'the presence of the Japanese provides an entirely new bench-mark for manufacturing in Europe.'[16]

Fordist mass production and Taylorist work processes were hallmarks of the modern era. If we have, as many claim, passed into a new, 'post-modern' era, it may well be that lean production and a less specialized, more flexible, and more responsible workforce will gain headway in the future. Just as mass production never characterized all of industry even at its height, and the exquisite division of labour and scientifically-defined work processes envisaged by Taylor never eliminated all other forms of work, neither are these two likely to disappear completely from the industrial scene. Behind them has always lain a very human, though deeply neurotic, urge for complete control, total self-sufficiency, utter predictability and extreme standardization, all in the name of a utopian desire for security and abundance. The use of rational means for mad ends goes back further than Ford and Taylor, further than Captain Ahab, and further even than Victor Frankenstein.

As the McDonald's chain shows, the offspring of mass production are numerous and varied. Agriculture reduced to monoculture, with goals of replacing natural processes and products with more readily controlled 'scientific' substitutes (chemical fertilizers for manures, genetically redesigned animals), is one example. Reports persist of hospitals in the USA where nurses must clock time like lawyers, avoiding any contact with patients that is not somehow 'billable'. Experience itself is made into commodities; it is quantified, standardized, and marketed in the form of theme parks, holiday resorts and package tours, and perhaps, one day, 'virtual reality'.

When Aldous Huxley wrote *Brave New World*, he dated its creation from the year of Ford's assembly line. 'By Ford' was the universal exclamation, replacing an older blasphemy. In this new world Taylorism and Fordism were present, not so much as explicit technical realities but rather as a hegemonic culture of modernism run amok. We have always constructed our societies out of the material at hand, dreams no less than tools, though the distinction between the two is not precise.

[16] Quoted in the *New York Times*, 25 February 1993.

Scientific Researches! — New Discoveries in PNEUMATICKS! — or — an Experimental Lecture on the Powers of Air

Chapter five

WELCOME TO THE CLUB

■ *But without scientific progress no amount of achievement in other directions can insure our health, prosperity, and security as a nation in the modern world.*

VANNEVAR BUSH *(1945)*[1]

Gilray's cartoon of a pneumatic experiment at the Royal Institution in London.

[1] Vannevar Bush, *Science, the Endless Frontier: A Report to the President on a Program for Postwar Scientific Research*, July 1945 (National Science Foundation: reprinted Washington, D.C. 1960), p. 5.

FOR STUDENTS OF science and technology, there is no more thorny problem than that of the proper relationship between them. Two basic hypotheses have been put forward to explain the situation today. One holds that, since ancient times, science and technology have been distinct enterprises, separated not only by intention and method, but by a gulf of social class and political power. Scientists have always been educated, and given both financial support and political protection by the power of church and state. The astronomers to the courts of the Pharaohs who could predict the flooding of the Nile, for example, or those elected to membership in the Royal Society of any great European nation. From very early times the names of some of these savants have survived, along with the lustre of their individual accomplishments.

Technologists, on the other hand, were the labouring masses, the innumerable farmers, cooks, potters, weavers, shipbuilders and craftspeople of a hundred trades who understood their materials and the processes to transform them. Some of these artisans devised improvements, some even radically new and useful, but since they were not literate their names are lost to history.

Not until the seventeenth century was it imagined that these two traditions might usefully interact. And it was not until the mid-nineteenth century that this actually occurred. The interaction was made possible through the emergence of new institutions such as the government bureaus in the United States or the technical laboratories in Germany. It was then that technical problems outgrew the inherited knowledge of craftspeople, and it was at that point that science gained sufficient intellectual control over nature to be of use.

The second hypothesis is based on the opposite premise. It maintains that science and technology have, in fact, always been intimately linked. The knowing hand and the able mind were possessed by a wide range of people: artisans sought to understand what they did and philosophers sought to apply what they thought they understood. Only in the nineteenth century did the twin social forces of professionalization and specialization divide these two, and lead to the creation of new types of institutions and practices designed to 'artificially' bring them back into fruitful interaction.

Part of the problem is that words change meaning through time, and even at any one time may well have different meanings for different peoples. Definitions cannot be the starting place for historical study, but must be a part of that study. The words 'science' and 'technology', for example, fall easily upon our ears in the late twentieth century, but two centuries ago would have had little of their modern meanings. The *Oxford English Dictionary* lists for 'science' a 1660 usage referring to 'a craft, trade, or occupation requiring trained skill'. The word 'technology', on the other hand, is listed as first occurring in 1615, and meaning a 'discourse or treatise on an art or arts'. Neither word reached its current meaning much before the mid-nineteenth century. Before that, 'technology' would probably have been referred to as 'the useful arts', and 'science' as either 'natural history' (biology, geology, astronomy, etc.) or 'natural philosophy' (physics, chemistry, etc.).

Today the situation is somewhat different. The power to define is the power to control, and the exact meanings of the two words are hotly contested by those who realize full well the prizes at stake. To define technology as *merely* applied science is to give primacy and privilege to science as such, and control of contested resources to scientists rather than technologists. If any scheme or notion can be successfully labelled 'scientific', it can, in our society, claim a legitimacy and certainty otherwise not so easily won. On the other hand, science can claim a large share of public money by asserting that it is the seed from which all technology grows.

Whether one sees science and technology as being entirely separate categories of human activity, or whether one simply places them at opposite ends of a continuum between which exist such combinations as applied research, mission-oriented research and engineering science, it is almost always science that is given pride of place. The phrase 'science and technology' rolls easily off the tongue, while 'technology and science' feels awkward and unnatural. But as feminist scholars have taught us, the choice and arrangement of words is deeply political. To say 'women and men' rather than 'men and women' seems not only awkward and unnatural but gratuitously controversial. To say 'science and technology' is to admit and accept the true and obvious, whereas to reverse the order is to challenge it. The prejudice in favour of science no doubt goes back as far at Plato's honouring of thought over action, and is still enshrined in western universities where scientists have a significantly greater status than engineers.

One final example is necessary. The term 'research and development', often abbreviated to R & D, has that same cozy and comfortable familiarity as 'science and technology', while its reverse, 'development and research', seems not only awkward, but at first glance oddly meaningless. In fact the order of the words is deliberate and significant because it suggests that one begins with research (science), and then develops a product (technology) out of that new knowledge. When one reverses the order of the words, one suggests that one begins with an effort to develop a product, and when a problem arises, one uses science to find a way around or through it. The first construction is science-driven, the second market-driven. While it is a difference of considerable academic interest, it is also one of profound significance to corporate or governmental policy makers who must worry about both budgets and questions of technological competitiveness.

When it was founded in 1660 in London, the Royal Society was called the Royal Society for the Promotion of Natural Knowledge. Though now known largely for the prestige it confers upon scientists elected to membership, it was, in its early days, no stranger to questions of the useful arts. A long satire in doggerel written soon after the Royal Society was set up, described many of the interests and experiments of the group. We are told in one verse that:

> A new designe how to make Leather
> A third Collegiate is now scaning.
> The Question most disputed: whether
> Since without Barke there may be taning,
> Some cheaper way may not to tryed
> Of making Leather without Hyde.[2]

A century earlier Francis Bacon had been advocating that men of 'science' should enquire into the workings of the arts and it is hardly surprising that this idea was taken up by the Society.

More fundamental to the new Society than its interest in technological subjects was the fact that it institutionalized, promoted, and legitimized the celebrated 'experimental method' as the one proper way to carry on science. Robert Boyle's investigations into the behaviour of gases, using his air-pump, epitomized what

[2] Quoted in Dorothy Stimson, *Scientists and Amateurs: A History of the Royal Society* (Henry Schuman: New York 1948), p. 61.

James Brindley one of the first civil engineers.

seemed to some critics to be an attempt to replace reason with technology as the mediating link between nature and understanding. Thomas Hobbes, Boyle's great detractor, held the derisory view that true philosophers were not 'apothecaries', or 'gardeners', or any other sort of 'workmen'.

But the honourable members of the Royal Society were successful in helping to define and canonize the practices and attitudes of what came to be called modern science. In part it was a matter of using agreed methods, but partly also of exploiting an aggressive attitude towards nature. Boyle himself argued against 'the veneration men commonly have for what they call nature, [which] has obstructed and confined the empire of man over the inferior creatures'.[3] Where the older hermetic tradition had found nature permeated with spirit, the newer mechanical philosophers worked to secularize nature and see the world as a great machine following the immutable laws of God.

As Evelyn Fox Keller has noted, the Baconian project for establishing experimental science was riddled with gender; Henry Oldenburg, Secretary of the Royal Society, stated that the intention of the latter was 'to raise a Masculine Philosophy', and Bacon had promised 'I am come in very truth leading to you Nature with all her children to bind her to your service and make her your slave'. Bacon believed that science could 'follow and as it were hound nature in her wanderings, and you will be able, when you like, to lead and drive her afterwards to the same place again'. Through science, and the inventions it might suggest, men could 'not merely exert a gentle guidance over nature's course; they have the power to conquer and subdue her, to shake her to her foundations'. This, it turns out, is where the use of the experimental method and scientific instruments come in. 'The nature of things', Bacon suggested, 'betrays itself more readily under the vexations of art.'[4]

In 1754, 'Some of the Nobility, Clergy, Gentlemen, and Merchants' of the realm formed a Society for the Encouragement of Arts, Manufactures and Commerce in Great Britain, which later received royal patronage. The 'Intent and Purpose' of the new group was to 'encourage Ingenuity and Industry', and William Shipley, a major instigator of the organization and an active member of the Royal Society, wrote to the ingenious Benjamin Franklin in North America, inviting him to become a Corresponding Member, which he did in 1756. In 1743 Franklin himself

[3] Quoted in Evelyn Fox Keller,
Reflections on Gender and Science New
Haven: Yale University Press,
1985 p. 54n.
[4] *Ibid.*, p. 36.

had tried to form a learned society in Pennsylvania, and in 1768 presided over the birth of The American Philosophical Society held in Philadelphia, For Promoting Useful Knowledge. The point of these various learned societies was not just to encourage the discovery of nature's secrets, but to aid in their employment for the betterment of society. In spirit, and even in method, they followed to a lesser or greater degree the example of the Royal Society itself.

The lines which these thinkers drew between 'science' and 'practice' were not so clear as some today would like them to be. Franklin, for example, designed his Franklin stove (to conserve fuel and to provide better heating in buildings) largely on empirical principles. He also, however, conducted basic research on the nature of electricity and was recognized by the Royal Society for his accomplishments. He turned his discoveries to good use by designing the lightning rod to avert lightning damage to buildings. Franklin was a printer by trade and it was a part of his public image that he was not just a diplomat and one of the greatest scientists of his day, but also a mechanic.

John Smeaton is best remembered as the first person to style himself a 'Civil Engineer' and as the person who, in 1771, founded the Society of Civil Engineers. He was also a respected member of the Royal Society, having been elected in 1753. In 1759 he contributed an important paper on wind and water power to the Royal Society. In his work he used something like the careful experimental method of science to derive what he called 'maxims' for the guidance of civil engineers. He stated, for example, that 'in a given undershot [water]wheel, if the aperture of water expended be given, the useful effect is as the cube of the velocity'.[5]

Because his father had been a practising lawyer, Smeaton's credentials were greatly superior to those of most engineers of the time who had risen from the working or artisan class, and his easy mixing with the Fellows of the Royal Society perhaps had as much to do with class as scientific accomplishment. Although Smeaton made his living out of what we would now call technology

Left: Benjamin Franklin and (far left) his model of the Pennsylvania Fireplace.

[5] Quoted in Edwin Layton, 'Mirror-Image Twins: The Communities of Science and Technology in 19th-Century America', Technology and Culture, 12 (October 1971), 566.

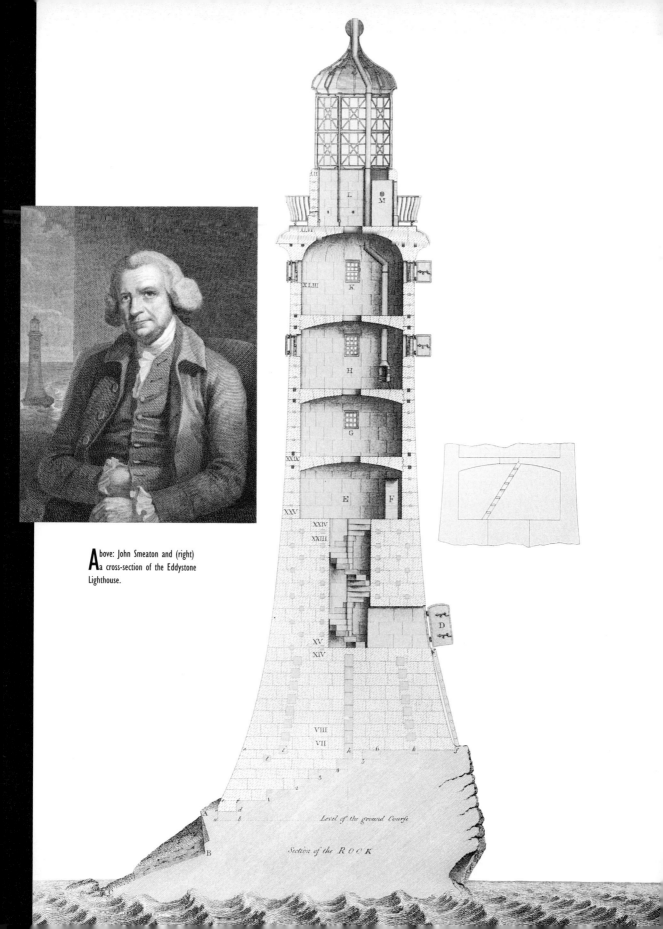

Above: John Smeaton and (right)
a cross-section of the Eddystone
Lighthouse.

Level of the ground Course

Section of the ROCK

rather than science, the same thoughtful, almost scholarly care that he brought to his wind and water power study can be seen in his perhaps most famous project, the Eddystone Lighthouse.

The Eddystone rock lies about fifteen miles off Plymouth. It once had a wooden lighthouse, destroyed by gales in 1703. Another was burnt in a fire in 1755. To offer protection against fire and the very severe wind and wave action at the site, Smeaton designed an ingenious structure made of stones that had been cut to dove-tail into each other. When grouted with hydraulic cement (which would set under water), the whole acted almost as a single mass. Built in 1759, the Eddystone Lighthouse lasted until 1882 at which time the base rock itself had been so badly undermined by wave action that the building was in danger of falling and was replaced. So proud were engineers of Smeaton's reputation, and so characteristic was the Eddystone Lighthouse of the best engineering practice, that its likeness was incorporated in the coat of arms of the Institution of Civil Engineers when it received its Royal Charter in 1828.

British engineers always placed a higher value upon practice and experience than upon formal education, and the great centres of learning at Oxford and Cambridge resisted any temptation to cater to the modern need for engineering training. A study of university students matriculating between 1800 and 1850 reveals that while only six per cent at those two universities came from families engaged in commerce and industry, at Glasgow that number rose to about half. This may have been one reason why it was Glasgow that in 1840 appointed the first professor of engineering in Britain, with the University of London close behind in 1841. Ever since the days of James Watt, Scotland had produced more than its share of eminent engineers and the association of the country with the profession persists in popular culture. Whenever a space voyager in the television programme *Star Trek* orders 'Beam me up, Scotty!', it is a piece of the past embedded in the future.

In Victorian times the vast majority of people working in mechanics probably generalized about their work. The rise of mechanics institutes, organized by mechanics and small manufacturers for their own education and general bet-terment, first in Britain and then in America, demonstrated a deep desire for self-improvement among workers. They worked long hours during the day and attended lectures and demonstrations, or studied in the libraries at the institutes at night. On the other hand many of the emerging scientists, whether practising physicians, school teachers, learned clergy or others, demonstrated a willingness to make themselves useful to the mechanical arts when the opportunity presented itself.

The continuing dream of applying science to technology was expressed by the young Joseph Henry in 1826. He later became the leading American physicist of his generation and the first Secretary of the Smithsonian Institution (dedicated to the 'increase and diffusion of knowledge among men'). In 1846, Henry urged that 'one great object of science is to ameliorate our present condition, by adding to those advantages we naturally possess ... But in nothing', he continued, 'do mathematical and philosophical principles appear more decidedly useful than in their application to the mechanic arts. To these they present in a condensed form the united experience of many ages; by a combination of theoretical knowledge with practical skill, machines have been constructed no less useful in their productions than astonishing in their operations.'[6]

The American scientist Dr Charles T. Jackson was convinced that science could be made useful, but was just as certain that scientists were not the right people to make the connection. In 1851, he told the audience at a mechanics' institute that 'no true man of science will ever disgrace himself by asking for a patent; and if he should, might not know what to do with it any more than the man did who drew an elephant at a raffle. He cannot and will not leave his scientific pursuits to turn showman, mechanic, or merchant; and it is better for him and for the world that he should continue his favorite pursuits and bring out more from the unexplored depths of human ingenuity and skill.'[7]

In fact, the people who helped link science to technology were many and varied. H.R. Palmer, the leader of those who formed the Institution of Civil Engineers, asserted that engineers like himself should act as 'mediator[s] between the Philosopher and the working mechanic'.[8] This opinion became almost a commonplace, but the engineer had to share that role with a new generation of scientists who sought to help, and profit from, the process of mediation. Chemists, especially, came to have a new relevance as industrial processes were reworked and as the science of chemistry itself improved its ability to question and interpret material phenomena.

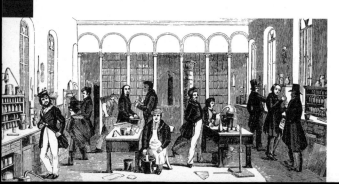

[6] *Albany Argus and City Gazette*, 18 September 1826.
[7] 'Dr Jackson's Address before the American Institute', *Scientific American*, 7 (1 November 1851), 51.
[8] Quoted in R.A. Buchanan, *The Engineers: A History of the Engineering Profession in Britain, 1750–1914* (London: Jessica Kingsley Publishers 1989), p. 61.

Left: Justus von Liebig's laboratory at the University of Giessen. Right: von Liebig at work on his condenser.

Perhaps the most celebrated of chemical laboratories was that established at the University of Giessen and headed by the French-trained Justus von Liebig. He was a strong supporter of the idea that chemical research could be a critical factor in helping agriculture and industry. A steady stream of students from all over Europe and the United States made the pilgrimage to Giessen to study at the feet of the master. Among these, from 1829 to 1852, were 65 from Britain, the largest contingent from any nation. No student was more important than A.W. Hofmann, the son of the architect of Liebig's laboratory When he arrived in 1837 young Hofmann decided to specialize in coal tar, a common industrial by-product that was the subject of some confusion and much ignorance.

In 1845, Hofmann was brought to Britain from Germany to take over the new Royal College of Chemistry which some of Liebig's British admirers had established in London. He was to stay twenty years before returning to Germany, and during his tenure he acted as a catalyst for the birth of a coal-tar dye industry in Britain. The instrument of his influence was his eighteen-year-old assistant W.H. Perkin who, in 1856, discovered a purple residue from a failed attempt to synthesize quinine. Perkin patented the residue as the dye 'mauve'.

Mauve was soon followed in the market by a French dye of a bright red, 'fuchsin', produced by reacting aniline, one of the coal-tar chemicals, with carbon tetrachloride. By 1862, when there were already twenty-nine synthetic dye firms in western Europe, such new colours as 'aniline blue', 'aniline yellow', and 'imperial purple' were all on the market. Compared with most of the vegetable dyes which they replaced, these new coal-tar dyes displayed bright, vivid colours which had enormous fashion appeal.

The locus for this activity, the Royal College of Chemistry, deliberately fostered the kind of entrepreneurial activities that Perkin demonstrated so well. He had lived in an area of London's East End which abounded with dye merchants,

■ *No true man of science will ever disgrace himself by asking for a patent . . .*

DR JACKSON *(1851)*[9]

dye shops, and silk weavers, so that the trade which he sought to help was no stranger to him. At the college he and other students pored over publications from the Continent, especially from France, for word of new developments. And finally, because British universities were slow to hire chemists for their faculties, young graduates of the college were encouraged to go directly into industry, where they found respect, remuneration, and exciting problems to tackle.

From the beginning, the transformation of dyeing had been an international enterprise. Hofmann had been trained in Germany by Liebig, and in 1859 Perkin's mauve had won a medal from the French Société Industrielle de Mulhouse. It was Germany, however, which worked hardest and most successfully at recapturing the leadership of the industry. Partly this was done by assiduously discovering and applying all the new developments taking place in England and France. More importantly, the Germans reorganized the industry itself: consolidation, a shift of responsibility away from the old-time colourists and master-dyers, and aggressive sales forces were all used to create a closely-controlled, science-based industry. By 1890, centralized and well-funded chemical research laboratories were a major part of the industry; and these in turn soon served as models for a restructured pharmaceutical industry as well.

The passing of leadership of the industry from England to Germany had several causes, among them a disastrous series of patent disputes among British inventors in the 1860s. At the same time, German unification in the 1870s created a strong, central state eager to involve itself in the strengthening of the new nation's industrial affairs. As a result, in Germany the state, science, and manufacturers all worked together in a powerful bid for domination of the dyestuffs market. British ascendancy had been based upon entirely new dyes made from coal-tar by-products. Now German scientists began to produce synthetic replacements for classic vegetable dyes, most notably for 'Turkey red' which had been extracted from madder roots by an elaborate process involving more than twenty separate steps. This breakthrough in 1869 saw the beginning of a highly productive and lucrative period of industrial research that included Adolf Baeyer's analysis of indigo in 1883 and culminated in his synthesis of the dye a decade later.

Liebig's laboratory was a critical factor in the training of young chemists who pioneered industrial research, but it was also important in the advancement of

[9] 'Dr Jackson's Address...', 51.

scientific agriculture. Liebig's classic study, *Organic Chemistry in its Applications to Agriculture and Physiology*, was immediately translated and republished abroad. His suggestion that agricultural problems, especially those relating to the chemistry of soils, were capable of 'easy solution by well-known factors', was as exciting as it was overly optimistic.[10] A Fellow of the Royal Society and distinguished member of the British Association for the Advancement of Science (BAAS), he was induced, by James F W Johnston and others, to submit a report on organic chemistry to the BAAS in 1837.

In 1840, Johnston, a professor at the University of Durham, was so taken by Liebig's agricultural work that he switched from studying mineral chemistry, dimorphism and resins to working on agricultural problems himself. Johnston published his monumental *Lectures on the Applications of Chemistry and Geology to Agriculture* (1842–44) and was persuaded to move to Edinburgh to open a laboratory for the Agricultural Chemistry Association, an offshoot of the Highland and Agricultural Society. Again, Scotland seemed to be more open to the application of science, in part, perhaps, because Sir Arthur Young, beginning in the 1790s, had already made that country a centre of agricultural improvement.

It would be a mistake to believe that any improvements made in technologies through the agency of science were entirely without cost. British fortunes and colonial jobs based on growing indigo were destroyed by its synthetic production. Old line-colourists and artisan dyers not only found their skills unwanted, but their positions in business firms undermined. Farmers persuaded to commit themselves to new and poorly conceived 'scientific' agricultural practices could find themselves facing financial ruin.

No better example of this could be cited than the much acclaimed 'Green Revolution' of the 1970s. Third World farmers were urged to adopt a new rice culture based upon scientifically-developed seeds, the application of chemical fertilizers and pesticides, and the use of heavy machinery. One result of all this change was increased crop yields, but other results were a shift from labour- to capital-intensive procedures, heavy indebtedness to banks, often using international aid funds, and severe environmental consequences: in short, the complete destruction of a peasant agricultural regime and its replacement by a scientific

one, deeply enmeshed in market forces which were themselves shaped by international powers and policies far removed from the soil.

Another example can be drawn from the increasingly important issue of standards. The establishment of 'standard practice' while not exactly 'science' in the grand sense, borrowed something of its method and spirit of rationalization. The most glaring need for standardization came from the developing industrial area known as 'The American System of Manufactures' or, more simply, 'armoury practice'. This system, beginning in the United States with the manufacture of small arms, but spreading rapidly into other kinds of manufacture, involved the making by dedicated machine tools of large numbers of 'interchangeable' parts. Critical to this fabrication was the use of jigs, fixtures and gauges to ensure that the resulting parts were indeed 'uniform'.

Screws were undoubtedly the most common fasteners in most machines, and their standardization was at the centre of one of the great technological controversies of the mid-nineteenth century. Each machine shop, on either side of the Atlantic, was free to make screws to its own pattern. As a consequence, there was no degree of interchangeability and replacement screws had to be made individually. In 1841, Sir Joseph Whitworth, Britain's acknowledged leader in machine design and manufacture, proposed a standard for the contour of screw threads and the number per inch for each diameter. As he pointed out, his suggested standard was a compromise: the average of the best practices then in use in the country. Since theory and principle counted for little, practice became the guide.

Whitworth's standard thread had flat sides set at an angle of 55°, with rounded tops and bottoms, and won wide acceptance in Britain. In the United States, however, William Sellers, in 1864, proposed a different standard. Sellers was often called the American Whitworth, though the latter was generous enough to proclaim him 'the greatest mechanical engineer of the world'.[11] Sellers raised three objections against the Whitworth standard: first that the 55° angle was difficult to gauge, second that the rounded tops and bottoms did not fit well into nuts, and third, that the whole design was complicated and difficult to manufacture.

This last objection hit the nail on the head. Whitworth believed

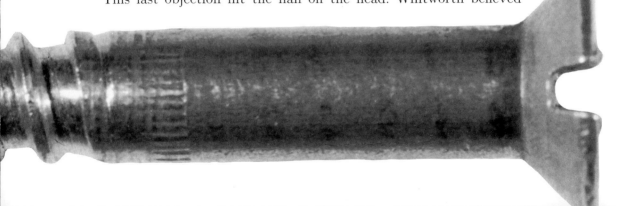

that, in England, screws were made by talented and experienced machinists, for whom the design posed no insurmountable problem. Sellers' thread, with a 60° angle and pointed tops and bottoms, was better designed to be made by what one American called 'all good *practical* mechanics'. The pointed ends needed fewer cuts and the 60° angle was easier to gauge. Rather than the 'good tools and good man to use them' assumed by Whitworth, Sellers envisaged the volume production of screws by 'any intelligent mechanic ... without any special tools'. As Bruce Sinclair points out in his history of the controversy, 'there was nothing theoretical or abstruse about it. It sounded democratic and it saved money'.[12]

The debate over mathematical averages versus production costs, and 'intelligent mechanics' without 'special tools' versus 'good tools and good men to use them', included an equally important element of commercial advantage. Most shops in Britain used Whitworth's standard, and the cost of changing would have been very high. Most American firms adopted the Sellers standard for similar reasons. The grand prize was the world market for machinery. National pride was powerfully reinforced by the commercial vision of having the whole world on one's own mechanical standard. National styles also figured in the resolution of the problem. In France, the government simply stepped in and dictated a standard. In England it was debated, but not settled, by Parliament. In the United States, the Sellers system became the standard entirely through the commercial choices made by individual manufacturers, customers, and private professional societies.

Screw threads were only one small example of the need for standardization that grew with the nineteenth century. Exploration and imperialism brought new areas of the world under European control. Entire new industries were born, often around the nucleus of entirely new inventions. International trade flourished as a result of both of these, and finally science itself was developing at an increasing rate. All four regimes depended upon standardization for their smooth working.

The fire that destroyed the British Houses of Parliament in October 1834 also destroyed the official imperial yard and troy pound, the standards set in 1758. The United States thereupon presented a set of American weights and measures to the British government and, a few years later, to France. In 1851–53 balances and standards were also presented to Japan and Siam. When the British government finally replaced its own measures, it sent a yard and pound to the United

Previous page: [10] Quoted in Margaret W. Rossiter, *The Emergence of Agricultural Science: Justus Liebig and the Americans, 1840–1880* (Yale University Press: New Haven, 1975), p. xiii.
[11] Quoted in Bruce Sinclair, 'At the Turn of a Screw: William Sellers, the Franklin Institute, and a Standard American Thread', *Technology and Culture*, 10 (January, 1969), pp. 25, 27.
[12] *Ibid.*, p. 24.

Right: competing forms of screw
thread from the Journal of the
Franklin Institute, 1865.
Below: Joseph Whitworth's lathe.

Fig. V Section of Wrought Iron Pipe Thread

Fig. VI Form of truncated Thread suited
for Valve and Lathe screws.

Fig. I
Graphic Representation of
Formulas for the pitches of Threads of
Screw Bolts.

The dotted lines show the usual best form of Threads of merchantable bolts

Fig. II Usual Form of Threads best Workshop practice.

Fig. III Form of Thread introduced Mr. Whitworth

Fig. IV Form of Thread proposed by Mr. Sellers.

J. WHITWORTH . & Cº.
MANCHESTER.
Nº 7. PATENT.

Above: Joseph Whitworth.

States. The new yard was found to be 0.00087 inches shorter than the old one, and was quickly adopted as the new American standard. In 1875, nineteen nations joined in establishing an International Bureau of Weights and Measures, headquartered in Paris.

The metric system was made legal in the United States in 1866, but was not widely used. However, copies of the international metric measures were received from Paris in 1890 and made the fundamental standard for length and mass in the United States in 1893. It is ironic that, having adopted decimal coinage from the beginning, the country so resisted the metric system that by the end of the twentieth century it still showed no indication of widespread acceptance. While America clings stubbornly to the yard (3600/3937th of a metre), and pound,

The standard and historical weights and measures of the United States Government in 1890.

Britain has abandoned them in favour of the more 'rational' French measures, including decimal coinage.

As emerging scientific fields rapidly developed into new industries, the need for novel standards presented itself. In 1893, an international congress was held, in conjunction with Chicago's Columbia Exposition, which established standards for the ohm (the standard of resistance), the ampere (current), the volt ('electromotive force'), and so forth. These terms honoured pioneer electrical researchers, but when dealing with living scientists problems sometimes arose. It is said that when a delegation called upon the redoubtable Madame Marie Curie, seeking to name the standard unit of radioactive decay after her, she accepted the honour but insisted that the unit be larger and therefore more imposing. Since the world's entire supply of radium was so small, and therefore amounts of decay equally so, researchers were for years plagued with having to use very small numbers requiring many zeros after the decimal place.

Not surprisingly, the Germans were the first to establish an official agency for the setting of accurate standards, the Normal-Eichungs-Commission in 1868 in Berlin, joined in 1887 by the more proactive Physikalische-Technische Reichsanstalt. Austria followed suit with its own Normal-Eichungs-Commission in 1871, and the Russians in 1878. In 1879, Britain established its Standard Department, patterned on the German agency. A National Bureau of Standards was formed in the United States in 1901.

The Standard Department did not obviate the need to create uniform conditions. The Kew Observatory, set up in 1871, moved beyond its original astronomical mission to become a general testing bureau under the supervision of the Royal Society. In 1890, the Electrical Standardising Laboratory was established at Westminster and in 1899 an English National-Physical Laboratory was inaugurated. All this institutional creativity reflected a growing need to rationalize a wide range of activities, from trade to manufacturing, and from science to imperial administration.

However, as the psychologist Donald A. Norman has warned, 'when followed consistently, standardization works well', but at the same time it 'is simply another aspect of cultural constraints'. 'Standardization', he believes, 'is the solution of last resort, an admission that we cannot solve the problem in any other way'.[13]

[13] Donald A. Norman, *The Design of Everyday Things* (Doubleday Currency: New York 1990), pp. 200, 201, 202.

As he points out, when the automobile first appeared, some problems, like difficulty of starting, were solved technologically, that is by the automatic, electrical starter. On the other hand, some problems were not amenable to technological fixes. Such questions as on which side of the road to drive, on which side of the car to put the driver, and where to place the gauges and operating levers, are those best dealt with by standardization.

From a technological viewpoint, two particular dangers hover in the background of standardization: being too soon or being too late. If standardization takes place too soon, one runs the risk of committing oneself to a technology which is still developing and may soon, in fact, be obsolete. More than one business firm and university purchased entire computer systems only a few years ago, and now find the hardware obsolete and even the operating system no longer used by any available computers. People who committed themselves to Beta video tapes and players now find that nearly all available tapes and equipment are VHS.

On the other hand, by waiting too long one not only can suffer commercial disadvantages but discover eventually that standardization is no longer a practical option. It would be extremely difficult and expensive for Britain, should it now wish, to convert its automobiles to left-hand drive and run traffic on the right, the standard adopted by most of the rest of the world. The humorous speculation about how this will affect the Channel tunnel highlights the need for and the problems of standardization.

The uneven nature of scientific development, combined with the varying nature of technological improvements present a picture that appears more rational and generalized from afar than it does close up. The telecommunications industry, for example, like all branches of the electrical industry, was science-based from its very beginning with the telegraph. It is nearly unique in that respect, having grown up out of scientific knowledge rather than traditional practice. Yet once established, the industry was only able to take practical root and enjoy mechanical improvement because of the work-bench and shop-floor efforts of skilled mechanics.

The historian Paul Israel has studied the contributions of the machine shop to the telegraph industry, and concludes that the 'relationship between technological change, manufacturing, and design' was 'central to nineteenth-century inventive practice'.[14] Since much of this was contributed by skilled and

[14] Paul Israel, *From Machine Shop to Industrial Laboratory: Telegraphy and the Changing Context of American Invention, 1830–1920* (Johns Hopkins University Press: Baltimore, 1992), p. 4.

knowledgeable workers, one kind of 'science', the practice of 'Scientific Management' or Taylorism, may well have actually undermined an important source of technological innovation. Shop-floor practices which de-skilled and disempowered workers, shifting new knowledge and responsibilities to new layers of management, took those workers out-of-the-loop, as it were. This made it difficult, if not impossible, for them to contribute to the incremental improvement of both product and manufacturing process.

Their place was taken, to some extent, by a new army of college-trained engineers, often organized into corporate engineering departments. As the scientific elite began to echo the prejudices of Charles T. Jackson and cultivate a cult of 'pure' science, unsullied by practice, engineers were in the process of

Above: Passengers and their luggage being moved from the broad gauge Great Western Railway to the narrow gauge London and Birmingham Railway at Gloucester in 1846.

creating what historian Edwin Layton has called a 'mirror-image twin' of scientific practice; a separate community of engineering research, in which something like the scientific method was used, but in which certain key values were reversed. Among scientists, theory was privileged and abstract thought was more highly regarded than application and instrumentation. Among engineers, the designer and builder were most admired, while the 'mere' theorist's esteem was low.

The engineers, taught mathematics and trained in science, nevertheless tempered their theory with economic reality and flattered themselves that they discovered and advocated the 'practical'. Engineers found themselves moving further and further away from the 'shop culture' whence they had come and moving into a 'school culture' which, to some extent, cut them off from the kind of knowledge available to the workers on the shop floor. As the mathematics requirements were raised and, recently, as computer-aided design has become available, there is concern that engineers are losing their 'touch' and their ability to see machines in their 'mind's eye'. If this be true, yet another rich source of technological innovation is drying up.

By the time of the First World War, scientific research, ranging from the most basic to the most practical and applied, was firmly entrenched in the corporate structure. No progressive industry could afford to be without its R & D laboratory, if only for public-relations purposes. The conventional wisdom, assiduously cultivated by corporate leaders and the scientific community, was captured in the motto of the 1933 Chicago's Century of Progress exhibition: 'Science Finds – Industry Applies – Man Conforms'. The centrepiece of the Science Pavilion at the fair underscored the theme: an over-sized sculpture in the rotunda showed a reluctant woman and man being pushed along by a giant robot.

It all had a very progressive ring to it. The secrets of nature being discovered by well-funded science, this new knowledge being applied for human welfare by modern industry ('better things for better living through chemistry', the duPont corporation proclaimed), and humanity being guided into a future of increasing ease and abundance by new technology. Sociologists coined the term 'cultural lag' in the 1920s to explain why social attitudes and institutions appeared not to change as rapidly as science and the consumer goods it was making. Caution, hesitation, objection, even prudence, were dismissed as conservative inertia.

If the First World War had been one of chemists, the Second was dominated by physicists. Their success both in developing powerful new weapons and creating defences against them gave strong support to the notion that, with enough resources dedicated to the task, miracles could be performed. From radar to the atomic bomb, and penicillin to rockets, well-funded and carefully targeted science appeared to be the key not only to national security, but health and prosperity too. In both Britain and the United States, wartime successes led to new post-war mechanisms for the public support of scientific research in the hope that a cornucopia of benefits would rain down upon a world sorely in need of new beginnings.

The benefits proved to be widespread, if uneven. Japan and Germany, as defeated aggressors, were discouraged from building new military establishments and so were able to devote a large percentage of their research and development effort to the innovation of civilian, mostly commercial, technologies. The less developed countries, often just emerging from devastating dual-economies (one based on exports, the other on local needs) imposed by a recently rejected colonialism, were seen as prizes to be added to the spheres of influence of either the West or the East. Large foreign-aid programmes, aimed at focusing the science and technology of the developed world on the modernization of the Third World, perpetuated the idea that improved technology was necessary for economic development, and that science was the source of all improved technology. Modernization theory (popular in the 1960s) was based on a scenario believed to be responsible for the rise to affluence of western Europe and the United States. The West also insisted that it was directly applicable to 'underdeveloped' nations.

The post-war investment in science was staggering. It was based on a curious mix of stirring references to goodness, truth and beauty, cultural aspirations, the nature of 'Man', and the desire to explore the universe, blended with vague allusions to a promise of technological 'jam' and better, more abundant lives. In the spring of 1993, an American government, caught between a deep recession and an even deeper deficit, could seriously consider pressing forward with the construction of a space station promised at no more than $10.5 billion ($8 billion having already been spent) and, at the same time, a Superconducting Super Collider with a price tag of $11 billion. In both cases, talk of 'experiments conducted in space' and discovering the 'basic building blocks of the universe' proved sufficient disguise to hide a striking lack of technological potential or economic benefit to any but the actual contractors involved in their construction.

This naive faith in science as being not only superior to other cultural activities but also paying handsome dividends in the end has not been without its critics. In 1966, after having spent $10 billion on scientific research since the end of the Second World War, the United States Department of Defense released the preliminary results of Project Hindsight. This was a full-scale attempt to assess to what extent that investment had produced useful new weapons. Innovations were divided into specific 'events', of which, as it turned out, 91 per cent were classified as 'technological' and only 9 per cent as scientific. Furthermore, a breakdown of that figure revealed that 8.7 of the 9 per cent was 'applied' science and only 0.3 per cent (two events) was 'basic' research.

The results gave support to those who claimed that funding science in the hopes of producing technological change had the same efficiency (and logic) as burning down the barn to get rid of rats. The National Science Foundation, the federal agency primarily responsible for funding basic science, quickly sponsored a study called TRACES (Technology in Retrospect and Critical Events in Science) which examined five important and recent technological innovations. By searching 'upstream' for basic research, without which the innovations could not have happened, it was able to discover that all five were 'dependent' upon science.

In 1969, two investigators from the British Department of Education and Science and the Council for Scientific Policy issued a paper, 'An Attempt to Quantify the Economic Benefits of Scientific Research'. In Britain, from 1972–73, the scientific research councils received £120 million, ten times the funds given to the Arts Council. The problem, broadly, was to justify this wide disparity, presumably on some grounds other than mere cultural values. More specifically, it arose out of the debate over whether Britain should join in helping an international consortium to construct a 300-Ge V proton synchrotron at a cost of £150 million.

The paper was critically examined by historians from the programme of Liberal Studies of Science at the University of Manchester. They were already studying eighty-four successful innovations which had won the Queen's Awards to Industry in 1966 and 1967. Using a gender metaphor, a principal of the study concluded that 'science is not the mother of invention but nurse-maid to it; that is, she helps innovation to grow up – and, moreover, she depends for her livelihood on making herself felt to be useful in that way. But she does not beget innovation, except very occasionally, illegitimately, under the back stair, so to speak.'[15]

In 1993, the British government announced what was characterized as 'The Biggest Shake-Up for British Science in 30 Years'. The year before, the first Cabinet Minister for Science in some thirty years had been appointed, and several research councils were reorganized. These councils together spend about $1.7 billion a year, more than half passing through the Science and Engineering Research Council. This sum is only one-sixth of the government's annual spending on research, and does not include the more than $1 billion given each year to the universities, largely for research overheads and salaries.

The motive behind the changes in agencies and procedures is the familiar realization that while high spending on science has produced excellent science, it has not led automatically (nor sufficiently) to commercial advantage. The judgement that 'the deep divide between the industrial and the scientific communities is often blamed for Britain's poor recent record in converting progress in science into industrial innovation' suggests that Hofmann and Perkin, with their Royal College of Chemistry, would find a welcome place in the nation's contemporary scientific and technological infrastructure.[16]

The crisis in the technology-science relationship at the end of the twentieth century is only partly due to a worldwide recession and the restructuring of world markets. There has always been technological change and it continues in our time. But, not surprisingly, its sources have changed through time and its generation is a process that, even now, is not well understood. In the absence of clear under-standing, struggles for cultural prestige and financial resources easily translate into conflicting interpretations of how technological innovation should best be fostered. For nearly four centuries now modern science has claimed to be the fountain which waters the garden of technology. There are sufficient dramatic stories of science-based innovation to lend credence to that assertion. At the same time, class prejudice and intellectual arrogance can blind us to technological contributions that seek to push their way up from the bottom, rather than trickle down from the top.

[15] F.R. Jevons, 'The Interaction of Science and Technology Today, or, Is Science the Mother of Invention?', *Technology and Culture*, 17 (October, 1976), 737.

[16] *Science*, 260 (4 June 1993), 1419–20.

Loading missiles for Operation 'Desert Storm' during the Gulf War in 1991.

[1] Quoted in *The Progressive*, 57 (April, 1993), 10.

Chapter six

WAR IN THE AGE OF INTELLIGENT MACHINES

■ *The Tomahawk is the weapon of choice if you don't want to risk lives.*

GEN. GEORGE CRIST. *(USA)*[1]

WARFARE IS ONE of the oldest of human crafts. Death, that great harvester of lives, is depicted holding his weapon, a scythe which is also a tool. The 'art of war' is a vastly older term than 'military science'. First the mechanization, and then the automation of the means of killing in our own time, however, have destabilized those ancient practices and rituals we call war, a transformation that has placed us all at great peril.

Profound technological changes in the way wars have been fought have taken place periodically. In the Middle Ages the introduction of the stirrup allowed warriors on horseback to engage in what can be called shock combat: the delivering of severe blows from sword, battleaxe, mace or lance. Without the stirrup either the inflicting or the receiving of blows would have been likely to unseat the rider, but with it, the violence of combat could escalate significantly. The resulting arms race pitted heavy weapons against armour for both horse and rider, producing weapon systems of great destructiveness, elegance, and cost.

Artillery too, especially after the fifteenth century, changed the form of war. In 1495, one fortress in Italy was reduced to rubble in eight hours by the artillery of Charles VIII, although some time before it had held out against a siege for over seven years. The new star-shaped forts of the Renaissance replaced the castles designed to withstand infantry charges, and their building, along with the design and construction of artillery, gave birth to the new profession of engineer.

In the seventeenth century, along with cannon, the introduction of the fixed bayonet established a new paradigm of warfare. Troops were now specially trained to serve in the artillery or in the infantry for massed bayonet charge. The training drills were literally inhuman, designed to reduce individual soldiers to

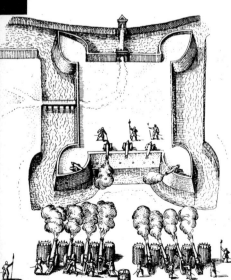

interchangeable and dependable parts of the military machine, mere cogs in the engine of death. Neither the eastern 'hordes' of Genghis Khan, the armies of Islam, nor the indigenous peoples of the Americas could fight in this fashion, and European hegemony over most of the world, or at least its maritime fringe, was ensured.

These armies were delivered overseas by navies based

Left: Gunners laying siege to a moated and fortified enclosure during the Renaissance.

Right: Carolingian soldiers depicted in the St Gall Psalter are shown here using stirrups which helped prevent them from being unseated.

ET SYRIAM SOBAL · ET CONVERTIT
IOAB · ET PERCYSSIT EDOM IN VAL
LE SALINARYM · XII MILIA

on the development of the square-rigged, multi-gunned warships, which gave western Europe mastery of the seas. The ships were the embodiment of advances in technology and they used new devices, such as the compass. This, combined with crews that were an almost industrial labour force, made vessels formidable fighting machines. The British Royal Navy, with its subdivision of labour, hierarchical command structure, methodical drills and ruthless discipline, anticipated both the regimen of the coming Industrial Revolution and the totalitarian environment of the Victorian prison or almshouse.

The American Civil War (1861–65) is sometimes called the first 'modern' war, in part because it anticipated so many of the techniques and technologies of the twentieth century. Conscripted armies were clothed in machine-made uniforms cut to standardized patterns and sizes. They were rushed to the front by trains; events at the front were observed from balloons high above the combat, from which intelligence was relayed to the ground command by telegraph. Troops, some of them equipped with 'machine' guns, others with rifles rather than muskets, fought from trenches. At sea, ironclads – armour-plated wooden ships – were already giving way to all-metal ships mounted with cannon in turrets. Under the water, the submarines made their first 'kills' in battle, torpedoing enemy vessels.

This war took place a long way from Europe, however, and despite the presence of official observers from all the European armies, the 'lessons' of the fighting were slow to be absorbed and applied. Count Zeppelin returned with the inspiration for his combat airships, and the 'machine' gun was partially adopted, but the span of a century without any major conflict, from the capture of Napoleon until the outbreak of the First World War in 1914, meant that any new ideas which could be taken from the US were applied only grudgingly and piecemeal, if at all. The revolutionary potential of the entire new system of warfare was dangerously muted.

If the high command of the armies of Europe were uncertain about the future shape of industrialized warfare, seen only in outline in America at mid-century, a host of visionaries, inventors, and imaginative writers were not. Especially in America, there had been a long tradition of imagining, and trying to invent, superweapons, at least since Robert Fulton's experimental submarines of the late eighteenth century. Late nineteenth-century fantasies tended to cluster around

A sixteenth-century German gunner aiming a cannon.

the newly-harnessed miracle of electricity. The 1898 thriller, *Edison's Conquest of Mars*, featured the inventor building a space fleet armed with his molecular disintegrator beam gun. In his 1871 novel, *The Coming Race*, Edward Bulwer-Lytton created a mysterious force called Vril, that was very like electricity and could 'destroy like the flash of lightning'. The 'fire lodged in the hollow of a rod directed by the hand of a child could shatter the strongest fortress, or cleave its burning away from the van to the rear of the embattled host. If army met army,' he warned, 'and both had command of this agency, it could be but to the annihilation of each. The age of war was therefore done.'[2]

Bulwer-Lytton's hope that this latest superweapon might make war too horrible to contemplate, and therefore, paradoxically, free humanity from the scourge of war forever, was widely shared. In 1891 R.F. Gatling, whose 'Gatling gun' was one of the earliest and most successful machine guns, told an inventors' convention that, 'if someone could invent a powerful electrical machine that would kill whole armies by the mere turning of a switch . . . there would not be a monarch

Above: A German naval airship which carried out raids over the Midlands, Yorkshire and Lincoln during the First World War.

[2] Quoted in Carolyn Marvin, *When Old Technologies Were New: Thinking About Electric Communication in the Late Nineteenth Century* (New York: Oxford University Press, 1988), pp. 147–48.

in the world who would go to war. He could not force soldiers to enlist if every man was certain of meeting death.'[3] The ingenious electrical inventor Nicola Tesla, writing in 1900, had a somewhat more realistic view of the matter. 'It has been argued,' he said, 'that the perfection of guns of great destructive power will stop warfare ... On the contrary, I think that every new arm that is invented, every new departure that is made in this direction, merely invites new talent and skill, engages new effort, offers a new incentive, and so only gives a fresh impetus to further development.'[4] And yet, even half a century later, the world's superpowers could base their hopes for peace in a policy called MAD: Mutually Assured Destruction. A new generation of 'geniuses', which had brought us nuclear weapons, could congratulate itself, perhaps somewhat wistfully, on having created weapons so terrible that surely war was now unthinkable.

In August 1914, modern, technological warfare was not unthinkable; it was only not much thought about. All the weapons of the American Civil War, plus many new ones, appeared on the Western Front, and the sickening slaughter of the Somme and many another battle showed how little the military elite was prepared for them. Repeated charges of infantry against machine-gun emplacements, however, represented not only incredible stupidity and callousness, but a stubborn and futile attempt to deny the industrialization of war. It may well be, as scholars have argued, that it was the mass production of munitions by the largely female workforce of Britain, and their subsequent use in vast artillery barrages, that won the war, but it was the machine gun that best epitomized the revolution in arms.

Although it played only a relatively small part in the American Civil War, the Gatling gun, and a number of other types of rapid-fire weapons, proved their usefulness and were adopted by European armies. In the absence of a war between the European powers, however, they were used mainly in colonial contexts where their true meaning was obscured by layers of imperialist and racist misunderstanding. When a handful of British troops managed to slaughter untold indigenous warriors, it was put down to the superiority of the white race in general and British civilization in particular. When a handful of Germans in a machine-gun nest were able to do the same to the Tommies in France, the British high command was unprepared for the result.

[3] Quoted in Marvin, p. 147.
[4] Quoted in H. Bruce Franklin,
*War Stars: The Superweapon and the
American Imagination* (New York:
Oxford University Press, 1988),
p. 205.

A Gatling gun made for the Camel Corps in 1874.

The cause was not stupidity entirely, though there was enough of that. The officer class in Britain, as in most European countries, was a hereditary one, which enjoyed and protected a craft as ancient as humanity itself. As one area of technology after another had been industrialized since the eighteenth century, as one craft after another was transformed and traditional artisans brutally refashioned into an industrial proletariat, the art of war had become an isolated island of skill and pride. Where else, in this modern world, were the virtues of discipline, bravery, perseverance, initiative, love of king and country, fear of God and loyalty to comrades still taken seriously and rewarded with success? Traditional hand tools and hard-won craft skills were matched, in theory at least, by ties of mutual dependence and respect, deference and *noblesse oblige.*

To the officers who loved belonging to this coterie and were rewarded by it, the tawdry environment and values of industry were at best unappetizing. The idea that a German conscript, from the dregs of industrial society, could, with a certain weapon, put to nought the brave, patriotic, disciplined cream of British society, was monstrous and unthinkable. If death could be mass-produced by unskilled labour, if the skills of war could be replaced by machines, then soldiering was a job like any other and officers were mere managers in the factories of death.

There was another, though related, problem. 'The army will make a man out of you' was no idle promise. Manhood was reproduced in war, as countless novels, poems and motion pictures attest. Women might bear children, but the rites of war made men. Turn-of-the-century literature on both sides of the Atlantic was full of concern that civilization was becoming 'effeminate' – weak, irresolute, soft, and passive. One oft-cited cause was industrialization itself, which took men off the land and enmeshed them in commercial values. War was a critical means of reversing that trend, replacing cold reason with passion, calculation with principle.

As it turned out, masculinity survived the machine gun, as the iconography of Arnold Schwarzenegger and Sylvester Stallone amply attest. The air aces of the Luftwaffe, the RAF, and the fledgling air arms of a dozen other nations swagger down to us still, with their leather helmets and white silk scarves. They had their descendants a generation later in Spitfires and Hellcats, and in our times in F-15s, MIGs and Apollo space capsules. In the United States, Air Force officers made it to the top by flying bombing missions in B-52s or engaging in dog fights with enemy aircraft. For those without this experience, even a familiarity with more exotic technologies doesn't have the same cachet. Efforts, for example, to replace expensive planes and pilots with remotely guided drones, however 'smart', are frustrated by a high command which clings to the faith that 'men' should fly machines.

Debates over the combat role of women and the presence of gays and lesbians in the forces touch deep cultural chords of misogyny and fear in the defence forces. The fact that 'manly' virtues like strength might be less important than before, and that others like bravery and intelligence might be shared by other genders, cuts deeply into the belief that war is 'man's' work and threatens yet one more sanctuary of male privilege. As more than one scholar has pointed out, new technologies, in war as in the home, the factory, or anywhere else, have the power profoundly to disrupt social arrangements and cultural values.

At the time, the machine gun, and perhaps the tank, seemed the major innovations of the First World War, but in retrospect the radio appears to have also ushered in a new era of warfare. Reports abound of the confusion reigning along the western front as armies of all nations used the new wireless to keep in contact. Troops at the front and headquarters in the rear were in radio communication and the babble on the airways sometimes must have confused as much as clarified what was happening and what orders were to be followed.

It was not until the Second World War, however, that a concerted attempt was made, in the words of the historian Hunter Dupree, to create 'an electronic environment for war'. The British work on radar began the new era. The electronic surveillance of the skies arrived in time for the Battle of Britain, and in that finest hour, physicists and electrical engineers joined Spitfire pilots as people to whom so much was owed. The microwaves of radar were joined by the radio beams from proximity fuses. The miniaturized radios that formed the tip of these shells broadcast waves which bounced back off targets, detonating their explosives as soon as they reached a pre-determined proximity. Since direct hits were no longer needed, more aircraft were brought down, and since the device could be set to explode at heights above the ground, their anti-personnel effects were devastating. In both the United States and Great Britain, physicists and electrical engineers were pressed into service to perfect radar, sonar, radio transmission and an entire new generation of electronic devices.

It is sometimes maintained that war is the greatest stimulus for technological change, and the twentieth century provides plenty of evidence that this might, indeed, be true. The computer stands as a case in point. Although analogue computers, using electro-mechanical movements, were in development during the 1930s, wartime created a great need for fast computations, especially of ballistics and cryptography. Operations research was developed to optimize bombing patterns and depth-charge deployment, and to assess the damage resulting from strategic bombing. None of the purely electronic computers were ready for use before the end of the war, but their availability soon afterwards reinforced the wartime commitment to electronics. The First World War had been thought of as the chemists' war, and both the academic field of chemistry and the chemical industry had flourished during the inter-war decades on the strength of that advantage. Now the Second World War presented itself as the physicists' war, and that, in its turn, became the most glamorous and privileged science. Both wars were won, in fact, by the blood and sacrifice of men and women in combat, not scientists and engineers at home in laboratories, but the latter decisively changed the nature of warfare for the former.

By the mid-1960s, the combination of operations research and progressively more powerful computers was beginning to change the way in which the military carried on its business. In the United States those with wartime experience, such as Robert McNamara, moved into the private world of corporate business, introducing electronic 'command and control' to the profit sector. From the Ford Motor Company McNamara returned to the Pentagon as Secretary of Defense and with his 'Whiz Kids', brought a new rationality to the planning and acquisition of what had come to be known as 'weapons systems'. One of his lieutenants, Adam Yarmolinsky, rather missed the point when he tried to reassure the public that 'computers can provide no substitute for the process of judgement based on experience. But,' he maintained, 'they can make it easier to acquire and marshal the facts that can be subjected to analysis.' Although 'cost-benefit calculation' was one important use for computers, he insisted that no one connected with that activity 'supposes for a moment that computer operations can take the place of human judgement'. The 'electronic revolution', he concluded, 'is probably more important to the military as it affects communications [rather] than as it affects the [function of] computers themselves.'[5]

A German machine gun (Maxim) in use on the Western Front in France during the Second World War.

[5] Adam Yarmolinsky, 'The Electronic Revolution in the Pentagon', *The American Scholar*, 35 (Spring, 1966), 272–73.

The problem with Yarmolinsky's argument was that it was, in essence, a restatement of that old canard that experts should be on tap, not on top. In fact, as generations of experience had shown, experts tended to come out on top if for no other reason than that the very decision to rely on certain experts and not others shaped the questions in such a way as to pre-select certain answers. According to the military historian Martin van Creveld, 'the bright young men who programmed the computers were not content to help run military administration and play war games; they demanded also to be given a hand in the management of war.'[6] The new rationality, therefore, was carried over to operations, not just procurement.

'Since intuition was to be replaced by calculation,' van Creveld continues, 'and since calculation was to be carried out with the aid of computers, it was necessary that all phenomena of war be reduced to quantitative form.' The result could first be seen in Vietnam where the chaos of a war against an indigenous people in their own territory, and in tropical jungles at that, reinforced an equally murky political goal. With no 'front' as such, and an enemy indistinguishable from 'friendly' forces, a sense of progress became as difficult to define as victory itself. The notorious 'body count' became the most obvious evidence of an attempt to 'routinize' the war, to reduce it to what van Creveld called 'an endless series of repetitive operations'.[7]

Meanwhile that conversion of battlegrounds into electronic environments, which began in the Great War and was so advanced by the Second World War, continued in south-east Asia. Elite scientific groups like ARPA (Advanced Research Projects Agency) and JASON, which advised the Institute for Defense Analysis, used Vietnam for the experimental testing of environmental warfare devices, such as seeding clouds to make rain, trying to create fire storms in the hardwood forests, and using Agent Orange to defoliate large areas of jungle. But it was the 'automated battlefield', advocated by guerrilla warfare experts, which was seen as 'the means for "stable war" – a relentless, relatively easy counter to the Viet Cong doctrine of protracted warfare.'[8]

The 'automated battlefield' began in 1966 with Robert McNamara's 'wall' at the demilitarized zone in Vietnam. This was to be a line of sensors which would detect any movement back or forth between 'our' side and 'theirs'. By 1969

[6] Martin van Creveld, 'When Technology Goes to War', *American Heritage Invention and Technology*, 4 (Winter, 1989), 49.
[7] *Ibid.*, 50.
[8] *Los Angeles Times*, 20 December 1971.

General William C. Westmorland had expanded the concept: 'I see battlefields or combat zones', he predicted, 'that are under twenty-four-hour real or near-real-time surveillance of all types. I see battlefields on which we can destroy anything we can locate through instant communications and the almost instantaneous application of highly lethal firepower.'[9] Senator George McGovern put it another way two years later, saying 'as our ground forces are withdrawn, Indochina for us is becoming as much a laboratory as a battlefield, with Asians serving as guinea pigs in our tests of deadly new technology'.[10]

The technology behind the notion of a 'wall', and then an 'umbrella', can be seen in Project IGLOO WHITE, designed to cut off traffic along the Ho Chi Minh Trail in Laos, and which operated from 1969–1972 at a cost of about a billion dollars a year. First, the area was seeded with sensors dropped from high-speed aircraft. Some of these sensors were exotic; one was disguised to look like animal droppings while another, a chemical detector, was designed to 'smell' the ammonia in human odours. The latter was foiled by the Viet Cong hanging bags of urine in trees to distract the sensors. The main reliance was placed on ADSIDs (Air-Delivered Seismic Intrusion Detectors) and ACOUBUOYs (Acoustic Buoys). The former plunged into the ground, leaving only an antenna (disguised to look like a plant) above, and then transmitted information based on ground vibrations. The ACOUBUOYS floated down on parachutes, landed in trees, and picked up noises.

When the sensors detected any activity in their area, this information was transmitted to patrolling aircraft which relayed it on to 'skilled target analysts' at a large computer centre in Thailand. These decided whether a response was called for; if so, planes were ordered to attack. The planes were guided to their target by the computer and their ordnance was automatically released. The weapons varied from large PAVE-PAT II, bombs weighing 2 500 lb, filled with propane under pressure and capable of clearing hundreds of acres of forest, to anti-personnel bombs like WAPPUM, DRAGONTOOTH, and GRAVEL.

Apart from sensors, other elements of the electronic battlefield included RPVs (Remotely Piloted Vehicles) or drones, which were used primarily for information collection. More important were laser weapons, the so-called 'smart' bombs. Although the Air Force had these available as early as 1967, it was not until the

[9] Quoted in Paul Dickson,
'Tomorrow's Automated
Battlefield', *The Progressive*, 38
(August, 1974), 13.
[10] Quoted in *Los Angeles Times*, 20
December 1971.

1969–70 campaign to interrupt the movement of supplies along trails through Laos and Cambodia that they were used in any numbers. They were, it was discovered, a marvellous way of hitting bridges, trucks and other small objects from planes flying high and very fast.

The 'smart' bomb was developed in 1966 as a cheap, strap-on kit, to be attached to conventional bombs. It consisted of a laser sensor for the bomb's nose and moveable vanes to guide it to its target. An attacking plane (not necessarily the same one that dropped the bomb) beams a laser at the target and the bomb rides in on the reflected light. Before the end of the Vietnam war new generations of more sophisticated (even smarter) bombs were under development.

A third area of electronic development was in the IBCS or Integrated Battlefield Control System. Covering everything from battlefront logistics and inventory control to directing fire from hand-held digital devices connected to main-frame computers, IBCS was conceived of as a system that would, in the words of Army Brig. Gen. Wilson R. Reed, 'electronically tie the sensors to the reaction means – the "beep" to the "boom" as it were – and leave the soldiers free to do what they do best – think, co-ordinate, control. The potential seems limitless.'[11] One thing soldiers apparently did not do best was die.

Above: a French Air Force Jaguar combat aircraft during the Gulf War equipped with a MATRA 400 Kg BGL (Laser Guided Bomb).

[11] Quoted in Dickson, 16.
Next page: [12] 'Military R & D: Hard Lessons of an Electronic War', *Science*, 182 (9 November 1973), 559.

One powerful attraction of the electronic battlefield was that it created a technological 'killing ground' where only the enemy, and not we ourselves, were present. It was reinforced by an old racist belief that 'life was cheap in the Orient', and that technology was the best way to deal with Asiatic 'hordes'.

The next test of 'smart' weapons came in the Middle East in 1973. In that year the fourth Arab-Israeli war in a quarter century proved to be 'the very model of a modern electronic war, fought with the best that non-nuclear technology had to offer'.[12] The conflict lasted only 17 days but proved to be an excellent testing ground for both American arms (used by the Israelis) and those of the Soviet Union (used by the Arab forces). It started badly for Israel, which lost seventy-five warplanes, about fifteen per cent of its combat-ready air force. As it turned out, defensive systems aboard the aircraft proved no match for the Soviet ground-to-air SAM missiles fired at them. The effectiveness of the SAMs, in fact, meant that Israel had virtually to give up the close air support of ground troops.

Matters were not much better on the ground. Here Israel lost an estimated 500 tanks, about a quarter of its combat force. Again Soviet-made missiles, in this case the Snapper and Sagger, which had never before been used in combat, proved deadly. Tanks, which were basically upgrades of Second World War models, were becoming enormously expensive with computerized fire control and thermal imaging for night-time operations, and their wholesale loss, like that of soph-isticated aircraft, suggested the need for some different kind of weapons. As in Vietnam, pilotless drones were suggested, but again received only a lukewarm reception. 'It's tradition', one outsider said. 'Tradition says that to be a general you have to command an armoured division. To be a pilot you have to fly dog-fights by the seat of your pants, not from some distant TV screen.'[13]

Less than a decade later, another test of new weapons came in the South Atlantic; ironically, this time between the weapons of western powers, not between the West and Soviet technology. In the 1982 Falkland Islands war a French Exocet missile (costing $200 000), fired by an Argentine warplane, struck and sank the British destroyer

"But what does a Strategic Defence Initiative actually do?"

158

Sheffield (costing $40 million). 'Smart' weapons, it seemed, had at last brought to a close the age of large, expensive ships. Actually, Egypt had sunk an Israeli destroyer with missiles as early as 1967. But coming less than a decade after the Arab-Israeli war, that in the Falklands dramatically confirmed the power of the new technology, used this time not simply against planes and tanks but the most expensive weapons platforms of all.

'Smart' weapons come in a wide range of 'intelligence', beginning with the simple ability to be radio-controlled to home in on a target. This type was the first to be used in the Falklands war when a British Lynx helicopter fired an AS-12 missile at, and hit, the Argentine submarine *Santa Fe*. The missile was launched from the helicopter, then guided to its target, which was being watched by the pilot, by radio waves. Even 'smarter' weapons were available, however, which could find their own target and identify it by any one of several sensing devices (and switch automatically from one to another), undertake manoeuvres to avoid detection, and sort out decoys from the real target. Such weapons are sometimes called 'fire-and-forget' or 'launch-and-leave'. The Exocet is such a weapon; that which struck the *Sheffield* was launched 20 miles away, came in close to the water covering the distance in 120 seconds, and struck without warning.

A wide range of 'smart' weapons was used on both sides. The Argentines had 'smart' mines which could discriminate between light and heavy ships passing over them. The Shrike, a British anti-radiation missile, could lock onto enemy radar and ride in on the beam. If the beam was turned off, depriving the missile of a path, the weapon could 'remember' the previous trajectory and find the target anyway. The Stinger, a ground-to-air missile, was described as an 'all-aspect . . . fire-and-forget, heat-seeking, infra-red weapon, with a built-in logic for distinguishing between decoy heat flares and an aircraft heat source'.[14]

Not every new weapon worked equally well and plenty of 'iron' bombs and Second World War vintage torpedoes were used as well. Some missiles, optically guided to their target by a pilot using the television camera in the nose of the weapon, obscured the target with their own exhaust smoke. The most damage seems to have been a result of the fact that British weapons and evasion devices were programmed to operate against Soviet technology, not against that of France, or their own British-manufactured Blowpipe missiles. 'With the proliferation of a

Previous page: [13] Quoted in *Ibid.*, 561.

[14] William J. Ruhe, 'Smart Weapons', *Military Lessons of the Falklands Islands War: Views from the United States*, ed. Bruce W. Watson and Peter M. Dunn (Boulder: Westview Press, 1984), p. 92.

country's missiles to many other nations,' one observer noted drily, 'it is desirable to program ESM [electronic emission interception and analyzing] equipment for one's own missiles as well as those of the enemy.'[15]

Despite the dramatic, televised pyrotechnics of the 1991 Gulf War, and the careful way in which good news was given to the press, more problems with 'smart' weapons came to the fore. High levels of accuracy and efficiency, it turned out, were dependent upon equally high levels of information. Despite a range of ground- and air-based radar, satellites and other sources, estimates after the war guessed that 50 of the 800 targets listed as strategic before the bombing began were later found to have been wrongly identified. The F-117 'Stealth' bomber proved to be 'difficult' to prepare for operations, and was 'vulnerable to bad weather'. It was reported that 'only 60 per cent destroyed their targets, although this was a high proportion of those actually launching their weapons'.[16]

A basic problem with 'smart' weapons was that like any other technology, they demanded a certain number of trade-offs. For one thing, the 'smartness' was expensive. There was a tendency not to want to use missiles that cost more than a million dollars each, or if they were used, to do so sparingly. However, in the early days of the war, commanders, uncertain of the effectiveness of their new weapons, sent several to the same target, just in case. The other trade-off was with payload. Sophisticated technologies to make the missiles 'smart' took the place of explosive payload on board, so that even direct hits had less punch than they otherwise might have had. Finally, some 'smart' weapons simply went dumb. The RAF abandoned some missions when one action video showed them a 'smart' bomb suddenly veering away from a bridge and hitting a nearby civilian area.

Perhaps the most overrated weapon of the war was the Patriot ground-to-air missile which was, at the time, hailed as a great killer of Iraqi Scud, ground-to-ground missiles. Within months the Israelis revealed that in each of the encounters they had been able to film, the Patriots had failed to stop the Scud warhead. Israeli experts were said to doubt that any Scuds aimed at their country had been knocked out by Patriots. The claimed 90 per cent success rate in Saudi Arabia was equally dubious. In the most tragic case, a known software bug introduced a timing error into Patriot operations which, when multiplied through many hours of use, amounted to a blind spot through which Scuds could pass unchallenged.

[15] *Ibid.*, p. 95.
[16] Lawrence Freedman and Efraim Karsh, *The Gulf Conflict, 1990–1991: Diplomacy and War in the New World Order* (Princeton: Princeton University Press, 1993), p. 313.

One did, killing twenty-eight American soldiers in their barracks. In addition to the British and other troops lost to 'friendly fire' (the result, presumably, of communications failures), these fatalities made it clear that even 'smart' weapons could do dumb things. As in the Falkland Islands war, however, oldstyle ordnance remained the backbone of the action. In the Gulf, only seven per cent of the tonnage of bombs dropped were 'smart'.

Most of the weapons mentioned thus far are the shells, bombs and missiles that carry the actual explosive materials. These, however, are often launched from 'platforms' which themselves represent complicated and 'smart' advances over their Second World War ancestors. The F-117 Stealth bomber, for example, was specifically designed to minimize the possibility of radar detection, partly through adopting an unusual 'flying wing' configuration. The instability of this design was offset by the fact that it was a fly-by-wire or computer-controlled aircraft.

The inherent instability of aircraft in the early days of aviation was overcome by a system of vertical and horizontal control stabilizers: rudders, elevators, flaps, and so forth. These were in turn controlled by the pilot, who gathered data by looking out from the cockpit, checking instruments, and generally 'feeling' the aircraft and the stick. The pilot noted and evaluated this data and then adjusted the control surfaces. In fly-by-wire, the pilot's brainwork is replaced by an on-board computer. The pilot still commands the controls, but they are connected to the computer, which checks the pilot's intention against other data it is collecting from sensors on the airplane and its environment. Only after registering, evaluating, and comparing these does the computer alter the control surfaces with its own instructions.

Today half the 'flyaway' cost of civilian and military aircraft lies in the electronic components and software; 'we like', said one industry official, 'to think of the airplane as just another [computer] peripheral'.[17] The first electronic flight control was developed by the Germans during the Second World War for their V-2 rocket. The need for such devices did not become critical until the advent of the swing-wing plane in the 1950s and 60s. Since the proper timing of wing-configuration changes was tricky, General Dynamics brought out its new F-111 with a 'stability enhancement system' in 1964. The next step was to go beyond simply augmenting stability and in 1972 the F-4 became the first fully developed fly-by-wire aircraft to become operational.

[17] James E. Tomayko, 'The Airplane as Computer Peripheral', *American Heritage Invention and Technology*, 7 (Winter, 1992), 19.

Today, planes like the F-16 carry four computers: one crunches the data and flies the plane, the second checks the first to see if it agrees, the third settles disagreements between the first two, and the fourth replaces the third in case of a failure. The technology has made its way into automobile design, where computers control fuel injection and anti-lock brakes. Complete drive-by-wire cars are even now being planned.

'Smart' weapons may have been developed first for use in the air and at sea because these provide relatively simple environments where complicated and delicate electronics work best. On land, as Vietnam demonstrated, 'smart' warfare appears to be more complicated. Part of the problem is one of imagination. In 1968, M.W. Thring, an electrical engineer at the University of London, speculated on the possibility of using robots 'to operate fighting machines without human crews'. Consisting of a computer, sensors, 'arms and hands', and a 'means whereby the robot propels itself', these devices could be remotely controlled by human officers, he wrote, and refuelled and re-armed by 'service robots'. He envisaged 100-ton robot tanks, armed with nuclear weapons, crawling inexorably across the map of Europe to deliver their terrible blows. 'Men will cease to be valued in battle; on the contrary, they will be recognized as a grave complication in systems design, introducing penalties of volume, weight, and vulnerability'. Indeed, it was the removal of people from the equation which appealed most strongly. 'Being a robot,' Thring wrote, '. . . it will have no feelings of fear or any desire to avoid its own destruction, except such reflexes as the designer may incorporate to preserve his machine.'[18]

The dream, or nightmare, of war by robots is an old one. Despite his realization that improved weapons led to arms races, not perpetual peace, Nicola Tesla believed that if people were removed from the battlefield by some radical new technology, wars would at least be bloodless. 'To bring on this result,' he said in 1900, 'men must be dispensed with: machine must fight machine.' To do this he thought it only necessary to 'produce a machine capable of acting as though it were part of a human being – no mere mechanical contrivance, comprising levers, screws, wheels, clutches, and nothing more, but a machine embodying a higher principle, which will enable it to perform its duties as though it had intelligence, experience, reason, judgement, a mind!'[19]

[18] M.W. Thring, 'Robots on the March', *Unless Peace Comes: A Scientific Forecast of New Weapons*, ed. Nigel Calder (New York: Viking Press, 1968), pp. 179, 167.

[19] Quoted in H. Bruce Franklin, *War Stars: The Superweapon and the American Imagination* (New York: Oxford University Press, 1988), p. 206.

■ *The Ro-bot sol-diers
spare no-body in the occ-up-ied
territ-ory. They have massacred
over sev-en hun-dred thou-sand
cit-izens . . .*

BROTHERS CAPEK, *R.U.R.*[20]

A tank after action during
Operation 'Desert Storm' in the
Gulf War in 1991.

[20] The Brothers Capek, *R.U.R.
and The Insect Play* (London:
Oxford Univ. Press, 1961), p. 40.

Tesla did not use the word robot, because it was introduced into the English language only in 1923 when the play *R.U.R.*, by the Czech brothers Capek, was first produced on the London stage. In this classic drama, robots are manufactured and purchased for industrial work, to 'save' labour by replacing workers on the production line. In Act II it is discovered that, in at least some plants, 'the workmen struck against the Robots and smashed them up, and ... the people gave the Robots fire arms against the rebels and the Robots killed so many people. And then ... the Governments turned the Robots into soldiers and there were so many wars. ...'[21] Indeed, it proves to be the beginning of the end, as robot soldiers massacre people without mercy.

In *R.U.R.*, the robots are deliberately purchased to be soldiers, and the manufacturer even has plans to produce them in different ethnic and racial models so that enmity, as it were, could be programmed into their behaviour. In the end, however, the robots organize and destroy the entire human race. Other robot stories also imagine scenarios in which robots turn upon their creators and wage war against them. Between 1963 and 1969 the Superhero 'Magnus, Robot Fighter' battled against rebellious androids who had violated what the science fiction writer Isaac Asimov called the first law of robotics, that they should not harm humans.

In one episode, technology has produced the expected abundance and peace, and human beings, no longer having either to work or fight, are seen by the disgusted robots as being 'a race of weaklings'.[22] What is significant here is not merely that the robots feel superior to human beings, but specifically to *men*. Like a generation of Edwardian critics before them, the androids fear that without warfare, males will not become men. War is, in many societies, a form of male reproduction, 'making' men even as it kills them.

The psychologist Carol Cohn sees 'the ubiquitous weight of gender' in what she calls the Rational World of Defense Intellectuals. In this world a kind of 'technostrategic' language is used, embodying the 'elaborate use of abstraction and euphemism'. The matter goes beyond 'hardening' one's missiles and 'penetrating' the enemies' defences, and beyond painting supporters of disarmament as irrational, emotional, unrealistic – terms that feminize and thereby marginalize their objects. Cohn believes that this technostrategy is 'based on a kind of thinking, a way of looking at problems – formal, mathematical modeling, systems

[21] *Ibid.*, p. 37.
[22] From Neil L. York, 'Comic Book Luddite: The Saga of "Magnus, Robot Fighter"', *Journal of American Culture*, 7 (1984), 40.

analysis, game theory, linear programming – that are part of technology itself'.

The comfort, even fun, of using mysterious acronyms, the masculine metaphor, the whole range of technostrategic talk, comes, Cohn argues, 'from characteristics of the language itself: the distance afforded by its abstraction; the sense of control afforded by mastering it; and the fact that its content and concerns are that of the users rather than the victims of nuclear weapons. In learning the languages,' she points out, 'one goes from being the passive, powerless victim to the competent, wily, powerful purveyor of nuclear threat and nuclear explosive power. The enormous destructive effects of nuclear weapons systems become extensions of the self, rather than threats to it.'[23] The ultimate result of this is that people disappear from the scenarios completely, and only nuclear missiles 'survive' or are 'killed'. It is the weapons which are the 'assets', and civilians become 'collateral damage'.

The notion that technology is merely an extension of human capabilities (telescopes allow us to see further, guns to strike further) is a common one, but the conflation of the human body and weapons of war has a special purpose and meaning. The exchange of human and technological attributes works both ways. Technostrategic language provides people with the words and ways of thinking that override 'normal' human reactions like horror, fear, and compassion. It is a kind of software to reprogram our humanity. There is an important sense, even, in which the army from earliest times has been seen as a machine, of which individual soldiers were only interchangeable parts. The uniforms, the drilling, the discipline and camaraderie are all designed to fuse individuals into a working whole which reacts without thinking and follows orders without hesitation.

'Smart' bombs, on the other hand, have been given the powers of sight and reason, to 'see' their targets and decide how best to approach them. Radar can 'interrogate' approaching aircraft or missiles and with IFF (Identifying Friend or Foe), can sort out those to be 'killed'. Robots represent the ultimate conflation of the human and the technological. The best of the first (intelligence, discrimination, rationality, the ability to communicate) is married to the best of the second (power, speed, reliability, absolute obedience, lack of emotion or conscience). On the other hand, robot soldiers, as either metaphor or machine, have always seemed particularly horrible, in part because they seem to magnify the worst of humanity and diminish what is best about us.

[23] Carol Cohn, 'Sex and Death in the Rational World of Defense Intellectuals', *Signs*, 12 (1987), 690, 707.

Three US Air Force C-123s spraying defoliation chemicals over the A Shau Valley in South Vietnam in 1967.

As we move toward an era of cyborg soldiers, not easily categorized as either persons or machines, we approach also the ancient ideal of the soldier: a ruthless, fearless, and efficient killing machine. Over the ages rites and rituals have been developed by men to turn themselves into such ultimately masculine beings, the very antithesis of the weak and feminine. Always the attempt to imbue 'smart' weapons with human attributes has been matched by a parallel effort to instil machine values and functions in the soldiers who must fight the wars and their leaders who must 'conceive' the wars in the first place.

On the outbreak of the Gulf War, early in 1991, the editor of *Science*, addressed the question of 'war and science'. 'Valor and heroism', he wrote, 'are the focus of novels about wars, but history has shown that, from bows and arrows to laser-guided missiles, technology is decisive if it is very one-sided.' He singled out 'smart' bombs and television as helping to make modern war better in some sense; the former because 'military installations' could be more closely targeted and the latter because of its ability to 'vividly bring to people the real horror of war'. But this is precisely what did not happen. Instead, television brought us stunning scenes of success by the seven per cent of bombs that were 'smart' and rarely brought to us the scenes of civilian and military carnage. The most technologically 'smart' of all wars appeared, as observers noted, for all the world like a video game, with the same graphics, electronic wizardry and lack of blood.

Concluding his observations, the editor of *Science* expressed the belief that 'science did not create war, but its advances can remove some of war's barbarities, can improve communication to decrease the probability of unjust wars, and can diminish the incentives for territorial conquest'.[24] The old dream, that new technologies could make war too horrible ever to be resorted to again, or so technological that they could be fought entirely by machines, dies hard. Writing in 1919 on innovations of the recent war, the Director of Chemical Warfare for the United States Army remarked that, in the autumn of 1918, 'some of our own inventions were just coming into volume production. A wave of disappointment passed over the Chemical Warfare Service when the Armistice came. One always likes to try out a new appliance under the conditions for which it was intended.'[25] It is a sobering reminder that wars are made by people, however much of themselves they have put into their machines.

[24] 'War and Science', *Science*, 251
(1 February 1991), 497.
[25] William L. Sibert, 'Innovations
of the Recent War', *Journal of the
Cleveland Engineering Society*, 11
(March–May, 1919), 279.

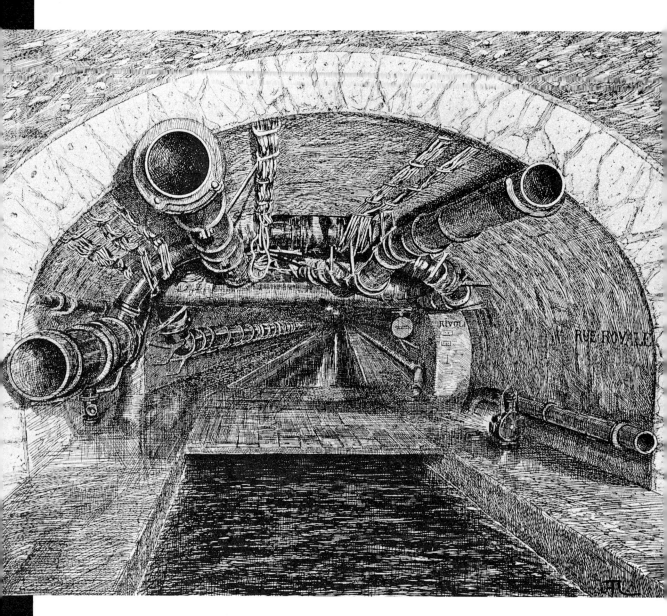

A cutaway drawing of a Paris
sewer in 1892.

Chapter seven

DIRT AND DISORDER

■ *The history of men is reflected in the history of sewers ... The sewer of Paris had been a formidable old thing. It had been a sepulchre; it had been an asylum. Crime, intelligence, social protest, freedom of conscience, thought, theft, all that human laws have prosecuted, was hidden in this pit ...*

VICTOR HUGO, *Les Misérables*

HE SEWERS OF PARIS are one of its glories, or at least were considered so in the nineteenth century. No one who has read Victor Hugo's *Les Misérables*, or perhaps seen the musical, can be ignorant of the fascination and fear inspired by the underground city, filled with more than one kind of human waste. The great sewer-building efforts of Paris, lasting for over a century, were basically an exercise in the construction of an urban, engineering infrastructure. At the same time, one can hardly find a clearer example of the way in which technology is enmeshed with other aspects of culture: fear of disorder, taboo and rituals of cleanliness, and the power of metaphor.

The monumental engineering of sewers dates at least as far back as the Roman *cloaca maximus*. Most of the great cities of Europe had made early provision for the carrying away of storm water and sewage to the nearest river, lake or bay. This was generally achieved by allowing the water to flow down channels in the centre of the street to a manhole, where it flowed into drains. Beginning in 1350, householders in Paris had been required to dig cesspits beneath their houses for human waste. When the pits were full the waste was to be removed with buckets and baskets by cesspit cleaners who took the sewage to suburban farms to be used as fertilizer. This same Act of 1350 made it illegal to insult the cesspit cleaners.

The open sewers and drains were bad enough, but the introduction of cesspits was worse. A pit of human waste seemed a poor foundation for a home. A half millennium after they were required by law, one observer in the late 1890s, denounced the practice of 'our forebears' in relying on such pits where 'they carefully kept an accumulation of putrid filth and a hotbed of the most horrible pestilence. It was not emptied until it was full to overflowing.'[1] Because the cesspit vaults were seldom watertight, their 'putrid' contents tended to soak the surrounding earth, creating foul smells, contaminating any water supplies nearby, and sometimes literally undermining the foundations of a home. When the overflow mixed with storm water in the street, the problem was distributed more widely.

Napoleon I began the process of upgrading the sewers of Paris by appointing a M. Bruneseau as Inspector of the sewers. His quite sensible task was first to discover what sewers there were under the city, and where they ran. Victor Hugo

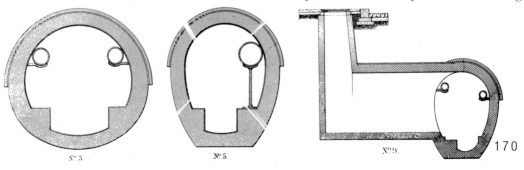

N° 3.   N° 5.   N° 9.

was struck by the fact that 'the sewer seemed endless and as awful as the *barathrum* of ancient Athens. Not even the police had thought of exploring this decaying abyss. Who would have dared sound these unchartered and pitch-dark depths which inspired such terror? And yet one person did come forward. The sewers had their Christopher Columbus. . . .'[2]

Once discovered and mapped, the sewer system was upgraded and extended as part of the modernization and 'improvement' of Paris. In 1830 there were about forty miles of sewers under the city. Over the next twenty years twice as many miles were added, despite the fact that, as Hugo put it, 'Paris is built upon a deposit singularly rebellious to the spade, the hoe, the drill, to human control . . .'[3] Under the Second Empire the Baron Georges-Eugene Haussmann, Napoleon's Prefect of the Seine, supervised an even more extensive building project. By 1870 the total mileage of sewers in the city had risen to 348. It was a figure ten times that in 1800. The sewers built after 1855 were egg-shaped tunnels, through which people could walk and along the curved bottom of which the waste ran, eventually to the Seine.

The new sewers were models of rational engineering infrastructure. Now they were more than waterways of waste; they were large and sturdy enough to contain two water mains as well. One main brought up river water to clean the streets and the other water for drinking. Another tube carried compressed air, telephone and telegraph wires were run along the sides, the electrical wiring for traffic lights ran along the roof, and a pneumatic tube for the postal service was carried as well. So elaborate and efficient was this multi-purpose sewer system, that detractors denounced it as yet another toy of the French engineering service, a notoriously elite group known for wanting to do things right.

Perhaps even more significantly, the new sewers, defined now by their process rather than their purpose, shed their old name *cloaca* (*cloaque*). As the historian Donald Reid notes, the term was derived from the Roman sewer built in the first millennium B.C. and had a clear anatomical reference to that part of the body where bowel, bladder and birth canal all emptied. This anatomically and morally loaded term gave way, at the beginning of the Second Empire, to 'sewer' (*égout*), with its more tidy and comforting connotations of modern engineering and social progress.

Cross sections of Paris sewer lines.

[1] Quoted in Jean-Pierre Goubert, *The Conquest of Water: The Advent of Health in the Industrial Age* (Princeton: Princeton University Press, 1989), p. 65.

[2] Quoted in *ibid.*, p. 63.

[3] Quoted in Rosalind Williams, *Notes on the Underground: An Essay on Technology, Society, and the Imagination* (Cambridge: MIT Press, 1990), p. 71.

Paris was not the only great modern city experiencing a rise in population, periodic epidemics (especially of cholera), the threat of rebellious urban masses, and a need to move vast quantities of waste out of its system. In London, the normal problems of removing rainwater and water used in cleaning the streets, and of dealing with cesspools and pit privies, were exacerbated by the introduction of the water closet around the beginning of the nineteenth century.

The use of running water in the home to flush away human waste appeared to be an unqualified improvement in sanitary practice, but it created problems of its own. Originally the W.C. was connected to the family cesspit; the resulting flow of noxious gases up into the room was eventually prevented by the water trap. The greatly increased flow of water into the cesspit itself, however, led to severe problems of overflow and soil saturation, compounding the need to find some better system than manual emptying of the pit on a regular basis. Although officials spent the early years of the nineteenth century insisting that water closets should not be connected directly to city sewers, the overwhelming burden on cesspools made such a course an attractive, and perhaps inevitable, alternative.

This vast new discharge into already inadequate sewers created an urban crisis. In 1847, Liverpool received parliamentary permission for the paving, sewerage, drainage and sanitary improvement of the city. Edinburgh built new main sewers in 1864. During the last half of the century London, too, found it necessary to upgrade its sewer system. The Poor Laws Commission in 1843 began a study of the living conditions of the working poor and called attention to the fact that unhealthy conditions were greatly worsened by the city's problems with sewerage. Some 20 000 people died during the terrible cholera epidemics of 1849 and 1853–4. While the germ theory of disease was not yet understood to be the culprit in such matters, drinking water contaminated with sewage was sufficiently offensive to be implicated in the disaster. No fewer than six commissions looked at the problem during the short span between the two epidemics.

Finally, Parliament, in 1855, passed a Metropolis Local Management Act which created a Metropolitan Board of Works to take charge of London's sewers. Sir Joseph Bazalgette was named chief engineer of the Board, and quickly moved to design improvements to the sewer system. At that time most London sewers ran perpendicular to the Thames, and discharged their waste directly into the

Kirkwood's water closet which was used at the Crystal Palace during the Great Exhibition.

river at the closest point. The resulting pollution created a major health hazard for the city as well as an unpleasant expanse of mudflats along the banks. It was Bazalgette's plan to build new, large sewers running north and south, parallel to the river. These would intercept the flow of the lateral channels, directing it to a point some twelve miles below London Bridge in Essex and Kent. The river above this point thus became significantly less polluted; only during times of substantial rainfall would the system be overwhelmed and dilute sewage be discharged directly into the Thames through the old sewers.

By 1875, Bazalgette's new sewers were in place. Thirty-seven acres of previously noxious mudflats were reclaimed from the river by a substantial construction along each bank, consisting of a wall to hold back the river and two tunnels. The lower tunnel was circular in form and carried the sewage south to Essex. Above it a separate flat-bottomed tunnel with an arched roof carried equipment for the public services. On top of both, a public footpath gave a view of the now much more salubrious Thames.

Because the topography was not always conducive to the smooth and steady flow of sewage by gravity alone, four pumping stations were provided to lift the sewage between 14 and 41 ft. The station at Abbey Mills used eight 142-horse-power steam engines to work the pumps and so impressive were they that the *Illustrated London News* declared in 1865 that they would 'exist for a very long time indeed, longer than anyone now living may hope to see'.[4] The paper was right: the engines remained in service until 1952.

Problems remained. Ventilation of the sewers, so as to prevent

The Optimus pedestal water closet as shown in S. Stevens Hellyer's 1887 publication, *The Plumber and Sanitary Houses.*

[4] Quoted in Charles Singer *et al.*, eds., *A History of Technology* (New York: Oxford University Press, 1958), IV, 517.

a build-up of unpleasant and dangerous gases, continued to be a concern, though it was noticed that the more vents were provided, the fewer complaints were registered. Bazalgette, in company with a Colonel Haywood, attempted an ingenious but ultimately unsuccessful experiment; a furnace was built in the Houses of Parliament's clock tower which was intended to draw up and burn off the sewer gases. The hot air from Parliament, however, proved to have too limited an effect. Although the air in sewers was unpleasant, there was some evidence that it was not necessarily always unhealthy. The 'toshers', those who made a living out of scouring the sewers for lost valuables and other debris which could be sold at market, were found by Mayhew to be 'strong, robust and healthy men, generally florid in their complexion, while many of them know illness only by name ... The men,' he confided, 'appear to have a fixed belief that the odour of the sewers contributes in a variety of ways to their general health.'[5]

In the United States, cities were too new to enjoy even the dubious luxury of ancient and inadequate sewer systems. In cities like Boston, New York, and Philadelphia, the nineteenth century witnessed a spiralling demand for potable water and sewage disposal, each reinforcing and making critical the other. It was a splendid demonstration of that unhappy truth about technology, that each solution causes problems. The stasis of colonial times could hardly be sustained in a growing and dynamic country, newly-freed of imperial rule and endowed with an astonishing array and amount of resources. The situation inherited from the eighteenth century was one in which urban dwellers, most typically, were supplied by a well for water and a privy for human waste, both located conveniently in the backyard of the dwelling.

Not surprisingly, the waters from the two conveniences sometimes commingled. Even those who received drinking water from nearby streams, from cisterns or ponds, could not be certain that their supply was pure. The 100 tons of human waste that New Yorkers deposited in the soil each day by 1829, for example, could not be kept separate from drinking water. The inevitable result was both unpleasant and dangerous. Yellow fever epidemics in Philadelphia in the 1790s (that of 1793 killed one out of every twelve people in the city) and cholera in many cities during the first half of the 1800s convinced many that something had to be done to rectify the situation. The first move was to go further and further

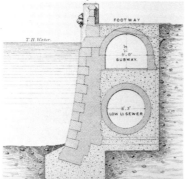

A cross section of a Thames Embankment sewer.

[5] Quoted in *ibid.*, 517.

afield to find drinking water. The example of Philadelphia is both instructive, and typical.

In 1802 Philadelphia opened its first municipal waterworks, taking water from the adjacent Schuylkill River and pumping it up to a reservoir with two newly-made American steam engines. These engines alone were an innovation, designed and supervised by the English-born and trained engineer, Benjamin Henry Latrobe. Following the lead of this pioneer engineering project, sixteen other cities in the country also built water works by 1860. As in Philadelphia, an increased water supply led to increased water usage. The per capita usage in Cleveland, Ohio, increased from eight to fifty-five gallons per day between 1857 and 1872. It represented an important leap in terms of cleanliness, but created a massive problem in water disposal. No American city of the period, when planning to bring in increased amounts of water from new waterworks, made any plans at all for its disposal after use.

As in London, the water closet was a particularly ambivalent innovation. Although known for centuries, and common in London by 1800, it came late to America, judging by the fact that the first American patent for such a device was granted in 1833. The opportunity to care for one's needs indoors, and in such a modern and sanitary fashion, made water closets one of the main causes of the great increases in per capita water use by urban dwellers. Not that privies were completely abandoned. As multi-storey apartment houses and tenements were built, they were often accompanied by ingeniously designed multi-storey (and carefully offset) privies. And as late as the 1930s, there remained thousands of functioning privies in even such important American cities as its capital, Washington D.C.

The clear answer, as in Britain, was to link the new water closets to sewer systems, but these were themselves rudimentary and designed only to handle storm run-off. Americans followed the campaign of Edwin Chadwick, the British sanitarian, who advocated the washing away of household waste by household waste water, and although his exact plan was never followed, the idea of water-transport of waste was widely adopted. Such an idea was significantly in keeping with the growing trends of modernism and that proved critical. The new system, when compared with the old style of cesspools and privies, was 'capital rather than labor intensive and required the construction of large, planned public works;

it utilized continuous rather than individual batch collection; it was automatic, eliminating the need for human decisions and actions to remove wastes from the immediate premises; and, because of its sanitary and health implications and its capital requirements, it became a municipal rather than a private responsibility.'[6] All these put it firmly in the vanguard of nineteenth-century technological progress. If it did not quite add up to the 'mass production' of waste, it at least defined its mass ellimination.

The first American systems for removing human waste along with storm waters were installed in the 1850s, and by 1909 the country had built 18 361 miles of combined sewer lines. Just as the establishing of water works had created a sewage crisis, the building of sewers created a pollution crisis. What they did, essentially, was to collect all the local pollution problems and create one extremely large one. Sewers, in the New World as in the Old, dumped their burden into the nearest river, lake, bay or ocean. And as late as 1909 in the United States, 88 per cent of that sewage went into the receiving waters completely untreated.

In Britain complaints from the residents of Kent and Essex, where the London outfall reached the Thames, had early led to treament of the waste that emerged. By 1894, some 500 patents had been granted for one method or another of removing waste matter by precipitation. These used chemicals, as in the popular A.B.C. process, which employed alum, blood and clay. In America, cities baulked at spending their own money to clean up water which was a problem only to other cities downstream. Sanitation engineers tended to support this view, claiming that it was more cost-effective to treat the water as it was taken out of the river or lake rather than when it went in. That way, everyone got the quality of water they were willing to pay for.

The city of Chicago showed more than ordinary ingenuity in solving its problem, which was almost completely self-inflicted. In that metropolis, human and industrial waste was dumped in the Chicago River, which emptied into Lake Michigan, along the city shoreline. Unfortunately, the city also drew its drinking water from Lake Michigan, and thus found itself recycling its own waste. City officials were forced to extend the drinking water intake further and further into the lake several times, reaching two miles by 1867. Finally, through the genius of the city engineer, Ellis S. Cheesbrough, a solution was found: the flow of the Chicago River was reversed, so

[6] Joel Tarr *et al.*, 'Water and Wastes: A Retrospective Assessment of Wastewater Technology in the United States, 1800–1932', *Technology and Culture*, 25 (April 1984), 234.

that the city's sewage now flowed into the Des Plaines River and eventually into the Mississippi, far from the polluted water of Lake Michigan.

The basic problems of potable water and water pollution have changed little over the years. New techniques of filtration and treatment, especially with chlorine, have helped solve old problems associated with human waste, though a number of British water supplies do not meet European Community standards and have been given extra time to improve. Problems of industrial waste are reaching critical proportions in some places. At the turn of this century it was still argued that acids from mine run-offs, for example, were quite a good thing in that they tended to kill bacterial contamination. The same can hardly be claimed for heavy metals and complex chemicals – many of these are proven to be severe health hazards but appear all too frequently in city drinking waters throughout the industrialized world.

Another burden was added to the system of waste-removal via water when kitchen waste was added to the stream. During the 1920s and 30s, in the United States, various kinds of grinders and mincers were installed at municipal sewage plants to reduce the size of large solids. Then, in 1935, the 'Disposall' was developed by General Electric for home kitchen use, though it did not become widespread until after the Second World War. The development of reliable, small and flexible electric motors, the low cost of electricity, the boom in housing estates development, and a general rise in consumerism after the war all contributed to the attractiveness of a device which could 'replace the garbage can, just as the vacuum sweeper had replaced the broom'. Another enthusiast claimed that the garbage can would 'ultimately follow the privy along the same road'.[7]

America had long generated significantly more refuse than cities in Europe. Average figures for the years 1888 to 1913 showed that while a sample of eight English cities produced just 450 lb per capita per year, and seventy-seven German cities only 319 lb, fourteen American cities were churning out 860 lb. Sanitary engineers in the United States were concerned that significant new amounts of solid waste in the sewers would overwhelm urban systems, many of which were already considered marginal. However, when in 1950 the town of Jasper, Indiana (pop. 6800) became the first in the country to require by law the installation of home garbage disposal units, new sewerage facilities were built to accommodate

[7] Quoted in Suellen Hoy, 'The Garbage Disposer, the Public Health, and the Good Life', *Technology and Culture*, 26 (October 1985), 762, 767.

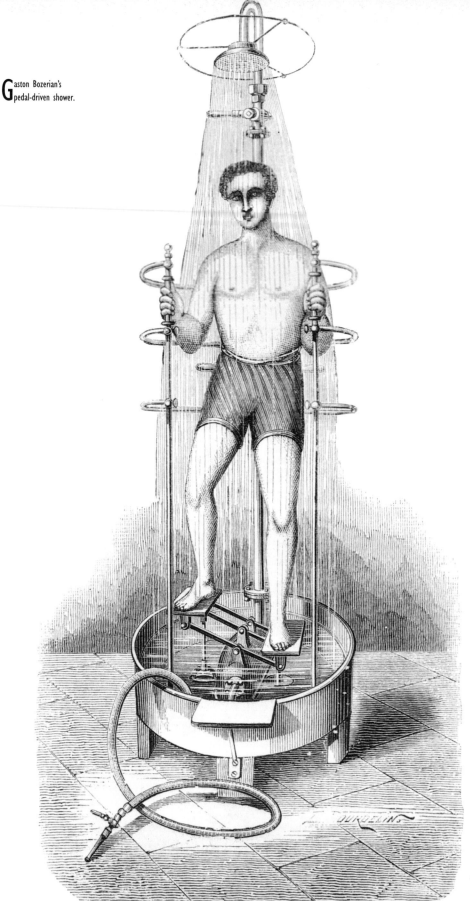

the anticipated flow. In fact, the town's plant was already in need of upgrading. Echoing alarms of a century earlier, Jasper had just experienced a cholera outbreak among the pigs fed by its garbage and, soon thereafter, an outbreak of polio. Not only human waste, but what humans wasted, turned out to be dangerous to public health and safety.

Fear sparked by periodic outbreaks of illness, even in the absence of a germ theory of disease, was closely related to the evolution of concepts of cleanliness, both in Europe and America. Greatly dependent upon the provision and disposal of large amounts of water was the practice of washing and bathing; it was a practice that grew from the casual and infrequent indulgence of a few in the mid-eighteenth century to a widespread and socially-determined ritual for the bulk of all social classes by 1900. The historians Richard and Claudia Bushman remark on the case of the comfortably-off Quaker merchant Henry Drinker who, in 1798, had a shower box built into his Philadelphia home. His 65-year-old wife, Elizabeth, tried it out and confided to her diary that, 'I bore it better than I expected, not having been wett all over att once, for 28 years past'.[8]

The convergence of cultural trends that led to Drinker's installing a shower in his home, and the spread of such devices (including bathtubs), drew surprisingly little inspiration from religion. Despite John Wesley's remark that 'cleanliness is, indeed, next to godliness', the clergy of neither America nor Britain seemed to lay much emphasis on the subject. Two hundred years later, Wesley's related injunction, 'Do not stink above ground', is teasingly ambiguous. Did he mean that the corpse will stink in its grave someday, but that people should not do so prematurely? Or was he referring to the human waste that was put into the ground, but not yet carried safely away by the great sewer systems to be built in the next century? Either way, such exhortations apparently played less of a role in the rise of bathing than did a growing desire for gentility.

Already in the eighteenth century, manuals which aimed at laying down rules for gentility were placing a great emphasis on cleanliness. Lord Chesterfield's letters to his son are perhaps the best remembered today, but others, like *The School of Good Manners*, published in Boston in 1715, were much read. Even George Washington made up his own *Rules of Civility and Decent Behaviour In Company and Conversation*. Like most of the manuals which appeared in America,

[8] Quoted in Richard L. and Claudia L. Bushman, 'The Early History of Cleanliness in America', *Journal of American History*, 74 (March, 1988), 1214.

his was largely copied from British models. As British polite society began to pay more attention to cleanliness, its American counterpart quickly began to follow the example. Even so, as late as 1800, one London physician claimed that although gentlemen washed their face and hands on a daily basis, they did not actually bathe from year to year.

Doctors appear to have played a large part in this development. The brisk, cold dips indulged in by some of the upper classes in the eighteenth century were intended to be merely refreshing. The warm bath, taken to remove dirt (and therefore ward off illness) was a nineteenth-century invention. Significantly, the role of the skin in removing waste from the body, was only slowly being postulated, but it formed a neat parallel to the importance of sewers in the wider context.

The technology surrounding bathing was an integral part of the process. The simple porcelain bowl and pitcher sufficed for the quick clean-up of face and hands, but not the full-body treatment. In 1891, on the occasion of the centenary of the United States Patent System, an American sanitarian noted that only one 'complete system of medicine has been patented in this country, and that was the steam, Cayenne pepper and lobelia system ... We can, however,' he added, 'show enough and to spare of inventions in the way of sanitary appliances, fixtures and systems for house drainage, sewerage, etc ... If good fixtures necessarily involve good plumbing work, we could easily make our houses safe so far as drainage is concerned ... The impulse for improvements in this direction has come mainly from England, where most of the principles of good work of this kind have been developed ...'[9]

The technology of bathing made its appearance in the eighteenth century, but as late as 1823, only 401 baths were discovered in Philadelphia, and these were not attached to plumbing but filled and emptied with pans or buckets. In 1829, the Tremont House in Boston, the nation's and perhaps the world's first modern hotel, opened with eight bathing rooms, proving once again, as the historian Molly Berger holds, that the American hotel was always a showplace of the newest technologies. Boston could boast of almost 4000 baths in the city by 1860, though perhaps most of these too were tubs without plumbing. In America the bathroom became available to much of the working class, and the number of tubs installed nationwide increased from 2400 000 in 1921 to 4800 000 only two

[9] John S. Billings, 'American Inventions and Discoveries in Medicine, Surgery and Practical Sanitation', *Proceedings of the Celebration of the American Patent System* (1891), pp. 413, 422.

Above: a bathroom from the Paris Exposition of 1889 showing a shower on the left, a geyser by the bath and a hot and cold shower over the bath. Right and far right: the two sections of a combined bathroom and lavatory designed by Doulton & Co. in the late nineteenth century.

years later. The often noted American obsession with bodily cleanliness was already evident. In 1928 an author of books for children explained to her young readers that, before the advent of bathing technology, even Americans had been as dirty as 'Europeans'.

Showers were the earliest popular form of bathing apparatus in Britain. The wife of the poet Robert Burns possessed a shower when she died in 1837; showers began to appear in the Victorian novel at about the same time. As water became more available, and technology improved, the bathtub replaced the shower in many British homes. Unlike in the United States, where the 'quick' shower remained popular, the British preferred the tub for personal bathing. By all reports and surviving evidence, for those who could afford it, the Edwardian bathroom was the epitome of luxury. It was a long way from the bracing cold dip.

As the habit of bathing spread, it became big business. 'It was the same,' the Bushmans assert, 'with every other aspect of cleanliness: housecleaning, clothes washing, yard improvement, street paving, sewage disposal. Each one required its implements, its chemicals, its machines, its instruction manuals, its mechanics – all in the service of cleanliness and sanitation.'[10] Soap, for example, became a necessary product for the proper care of the body. The trade had traditionally been divided into two branches: toilet soap, the manufacture of which was dominated by the French, was a branch of the perfume business. Laundry soap, on the other hand, grew out of the slaughter house industry, drawing, as it did, upon the waste tallow for its main ingredient.

By mid-nineteenth century, however, soap for bathing was in demand and in 1851, at the Crystal Palace Exhibition in London, over 700 soap entries were exhibited. Great Britain lifted its excise tax on soap two years later. In the 1880s the Procter and Gamble company of America brought out its famous Ivory soap in the large bar format familiar as laundry soap, but it was notched so that it could be broken into two smaller bars making it suitable for bathing. It was, the company advertised, 'so perfectly made that there is no better for the toilet and bath, and it is sold at such a reasonable price that it can be used economically in the laundry'.[11]

The process of doing the laundry was changing as well. The historian Arwen Mohun, in comparing the rise of steam laundries in Britain and the United States,

An advert for Cherry Blossom soap which appeared in the Christmas edition of *The Sketch* in 1893.

[10] Bushman and Bushman, 1232–3.
[11] Quoted in *ibid.*, 1236.

has noted the link between the construction of middle-class notions of cleanliness, the growth of Victorian cities with their water and sewerage works, and the urge to industrialize the cleaning of clothing. As she points out, 'among the most prominent public symbols of these new-found values was the clean, white, starched and ironed shirt. Its careful preparation and presentation in public places preserved two important illusions for the middle class: it hid the fact that one worked for a living and preserved the appearance that one had transcended animality by concealing evidence of bodily functions such as perspiration.'[12] Hence the conclusion that if cleanliness suggested propriety and gentility, then impropriety suggested filth. One writer warned in 1859 that, 'when you come across a lady who delights in talking scandal, in telling the world of all the wickedness she knows there is in it, quietly mark it down in your memorandum book, that she is addicted to the wearing of dirty linen'.[13]

The great steam laundries of the late nineteenth century, with their water boilers and mangles, washers, extractors, centrifuges and drying rooms, strong soaps and caustics, dangerous work and long hours, multiplied rapidly in the urban environment. By 1903, there were at least 403 in Chicago and in London whole districts were characterized by the laundry. Not only did the metropolis provide the means for bringing in and taking away the vast quantities of water the steam laundries required, but the filth of the city made industrial laundries almost necessary. The 1877 servant's manual *The Laundry Maid* warned that, 'it is necessary for the London laundry woman, whatever her station, to remember that clothes become dirtier much sooner, or much dirtier with the same amount of wear, in London than in the country'.[14]

The war against dirt, then, whether flushed off the skin in a bath or down the commode in a water closet, was fully engaged, if not yet won by 1900. Perhaps it was not entirely for the efficiency of plumbing that the toilet and the bathtub were often placed together in the same room, at least in America. In other countries, as in Australia, they are just as often placed in separate rooms. There one very much gets the impression that the privy, still to be found occasionally at the back of the yard, has been allowed, transformed, just inside the back of the house but no further, while the civilizing influence of the bath is welcomed next to the bedroom.

Right: Burrell's small Alpha washing machine showing the dasher in the centre to agitate the washing. Far right: Thomas Bradford's washing machine in which clothes were supported by rubber rollers.

The anthropologist Mary Douglas says that 'pollution beliefs protect the most vulnerable domains, where ambiguity would most weaken the fragile structure'.[15] Her argument is that, for many cultures (perhaps including our own), good order and social stability require the strict respect of boundaries and that violations of these borders, as in Lord Chesterfield's definition of dirt as matter out of place, risk social and spiritual chaos. She suggests that, for us, dirt 'is a kind of compendium category for all events which blur, smudge, contradict, or otherwise confuse accepted classifications'.[16] The cultural ambiguity implied by these threats to order are dealt with by avoidance, discrimination and pressure to conform.

Above: coppers in Chauvet's model laundry in Paris in 1904.

Previous page: [12] Arwen Palmer Mohun, 'Women, Work, and Technology: The Steam Laundry in the United States and Great Britain', 1880–1920 (PhD dissertation, History, Case Western Reserve University, 1992), pp. 42–43.
[13] Quoted in *ibid.*, pp. 43–44.

[14] Quoted in *ibid.*, p. 46.
[15] Mary Douglas, 'Pollution', in *Implicit Meanings: Essays in Anthropology* (London: Routledge, 1975), p. 58.

[16] *Ibid.*, p. 51.

Most importantly, avoidance requires that contact should not be made with products from the body: blood, urine, spit etc. Such contact represents others, of a social or political nature, that might contaminate. 'We would,' she writes, 'expect to find pollution concepts guarding threatened disturbances of the social order', and so it is in our society. One is tempted, for example, to see the current avoidance of the blood and other fluids of people with AIDS as having a base not only in the isolation from disease but also, symbolically, from the 'transgressive' categories of homosexual and drug addict.[17]

This suggests, as well, that the concern for great sewer projects in nineteenth-century Paris, London and other great metropolises was a reaction not only against the contagion of cholera and other diseases (the causes of which, at any rate, were misunderstood) but the contagion of social dislocation and moral collapse. It is not a coincidence that, when Dr Parent-Duchatelet published his pioneering study of the prostitutes of Paris in 1836, he made explicit reference to his previous report of the city's sewers and drew a parallel between the two institutions. It was the century in which the image of Paris was sexualized, and the metropolis itself was often depicted as a harlot, offering pleasures unspoken, but at the same time threatening disease of the body and soul.

Paris, however, was the city not only of sexual freedom but also of revolution. It has been suggested, perhaps half in jest, that London was free of revolution during the nineteenth century because its streets, unlike those of Paris, were not paved with cobble stones which could so easily be prised and used for missiles. For whatever reason, republics and empires followed one another with startling regularity in Paris and the *cloaca* of the city was symbolically implicated in them all. That underground city, unmapped, uncontrolled and filled with filth, became a powerful metaphor for the transgression of the political, social and moral orders above ground. Above as below, the scum of society could break the rules, plot disorder and live outside 'normal' society.

Just as Paris itself was feminine, so were its sewers. The stew of urine and faeces, semen and too often the bodies of stillborn or murdered babies seemed much more the work of nature than of civilization; nature out of control, in its most natural state. Just as female nature was always a threat to male structure, privilege and order, and had to be severely controlled by patriarchal rule, so the sewers needed to

[17] *Ibid.*, p. 55.

be brought under control, to be well-regulated so that the inevitable results of human 'nature' could be channelled away harmlessly. As Donald Reid suggests, the sewers of Victorian cities were contested terrain, to be reclaimed from nature and brought under male domination. No masculine coding could compete with engineering rationality.

The extraordinary tour of the sewers of Paris, which began in 1867, continues today. This 'second, subterranean Paris', after the engineering work of decades, could boast an architecture as interesting in its own way as any in the Paris on the surface. At that time visitors went down by a staircase and went through the tunnels in deluxe versions of the wagons and boats used for cleaning by the sewermen. The wagons and boats were pulled by the sewermen themselves and during the hour-long trip only the water appeared dirty, the rest clean, efficient, and undeniably modern. Women, who were once associated with the natural disorder of the *cloaca*, were now welcomed to the rationalized and masculinized sewers as visitors. Ladies could participate in the tours 'without fatigue or fear of anything not clean', and an American visitor remarked that 'the presence of lovely women can add a charm to the sewer'.[18] Now they provided not a reminder of the dangers of the sewer, but a marked contrast to their masculinity. One was more likely to see police agents than criminals.

The felt need of privileged society in the nineteenth century somehow to gain control of their great cities, was not limited to the sewers. As Elizabeth Wilson has suggested, efficient sewage systems were as desperately needed as adequate water supplies. In both cases, morality was inextricably linked with cleanliness, disorder with filth. For the Victorians excretion became a metaphor and a symbol for moral filth, perhaps even for the working class itself; when they spoke and

Above: a group gathering for a tour of Paris sewers in 1892.

[18] Quoted in Donald Reid *Paris Sewers and Sewermen: Realities and Representations* (Cambridge: Harvard University Press, 1991), p. 41.

wrote of the 'cleansing of the city of filth, refuse and dung,' they may really have longed to rid the cities of the labouring poor altogether.[19]

When George Godwin, writing of the sewage problem of London in 1854, said that, 'from the polluted bosom of the river steams up, incessantly though unseen, the vapours of a retributive poison', he spoke in terms that could have meaning for the Los Angeles of the 1990s, with its barrios and ghettos of hopelessness and resentment, or a hundred other cities in the more than a hundred years since Godwin's time.[20] In Fritz Lang's film, *Metropolis*, the city lives in layers, with the ruling class on the highest level. Underground lies the machinery that performs the city's work. Beneath that, at the lowest level, dwell the workers of Metropolis, degraded by exhausting and alienated toil below the city. When the master of the city gains control of the technology for making robots, he realizes that his workers are now simply a liability. He provokes them to blind and violent rebellion, in which they stop the machines and flood their own quarters, threatening to drown the children left behind. To be flushed out of the city through their own underground channels is the fate of the brutal and brutalized lower (lowest) orders.

At a 'deeper' level, the fascination with and fear of an underclass taps into the rich mythic power of the underground in our culture. The historian Rosalind Williams has traced the imaginative uses to which we have put the technological and social purpose of getting 'beneath the surface' to those places where truth is thought most obviously to lie: 'the subterranean environment is a technological one – but it is also a mental landscape, a social terrain, and an ideological map'.[21]

The underground is made, not given; it represents what people choose to do rather than what they must. If, as innumerable critics have charged, it was the fate of modernity to see the natural displaced by the artificial, the organic by the inorganic, and change by the planned, then the underground provided a picture of the future – of the kind of world modern people would build if they had the chance. Many modern authors, such as Aldous Huxley in *Brave New World* (1932), used the city as the model for the future, but the city underground was even more stark. In the nineteenth and early twentieth centuries such imaginative writers as H.G. Wells and Jules Verne set novels of dystopia deep under the earth.

As Williams points out, as science advanced during the nineteenth century, the possibility of finding some hidden world under the ground became less and

[19] Elizabeth Wilson, *The Sphinx in the City: Urban Life, the Control of Disorder, and Women* (Berkeley: University of California Press, 1991), p. 37.
[20] Quoted in *ibid.*

[21] Quoted in Rosalind Williams, *Notes on the Underground: An Essay on Technology, Society, and the Imagination* (Cambridge: MIT Press, 1990) p. 21.

Above: a view of Metropolis, the city in Fritz Lang's film of the same name. Below: underground in Metropolis where the machinery performs the work of the city.

less likely, although the United States Congress financed an exploratory expedition to the South Pole as late as 1838, partly due to John Cleves Symmes' theory that underground worlds existed. At the same time technology was making the possibility of creating underground worlds ever more feasible. It was a great age of tunnels, mines, and subways as well as of sewers.

What might happen in the technological future was the subject of E.M. Forster's short story *The Machine Stops*, written in reaction, as he said, 'to one of the earlier heavens of H.G. Wells'.[22] In this story, each person lives underground in 'a small room, hexagonal in shape like the cell of a bee. It is lighted neither by window nor by lamp', but is aglow nonetheless; fresh air is brought in, though the vent is not visible. In short, the room is completely sealed off from 'nature', but its occupant is supplied with everything needed, from heat to food, entertainment to social contact (by way of electrical communication). Our protagonist lives in such a room, as does his mother, whose room, 'though it contains nothing, was in touch with all that she cared for in the world'. She lived, in *post*-modern terms, in a 'virtual' world. Her son, our hero, longs to see the surface of the earth, and to father a child. Both these 'natural' rights are denied to him, though he does briefly find his way to the earth's surface through a protruding 'vomitory'.

Finally, The Machine that keeps the whole human race alive beneath the earth, fails, and one by one the life-support systems fail. His mother, who had 'felt the delirium of acquiescence', was more accepting of her life than he, who had felt the 'terrors of direct experience'. Now, as life became unmanageable, the hero weeps for 'the sin against the body ... the centuries of wrong against the muscles and the nerves, and those five portals by which we can alone apprehend ...'[23]

It was a powerful, though probably not deliberate, answer to Mrs Frances Trollope who, in the 1830s, had noted that the English, as opposed to the French, had become more fastidious in their tolerance of experience: 'When we cease to hear, see, and smell things which are disagreeable, it is natural that we should cease to speak of them; and it is, I believe, quite certain, that the English take more pains than any other people in the world that the senses – those conductors of sensation from the body to the soul – shall convey to the spirit as little disagreeable intelligence of what befalls the case in which it dwells, as possible'.[24]

[22] Author's introduction to E. M. Forster, *Collected Short Stories* (London: Sidgwick and Jackson, 1947), p. 6.
[23] *Ibid.*, p. 145.
[24] Quoted in Donald Reid *Paris Sewers and Sewermen* (Cambridge: Harvard University Press, 1991), p. 37.

The sewers of Paris, London and a host of other cities during the nineteenth century, were deeply implicated in the political and social discourses of their time. The great modern cities spawned by the Industrial Revolution were both models and markers of the modernist attempt to centralize power, extend it over peoples at the margin at home and abroad, and most particularly to invoke the power and prestige of science in that project. All over the world nature was conquered and disciplined, and even the cities, which at first glance appeared to be the very epitome of the artificial and constructed, were perceived to be feminine organisms: wastelands in some accounts, wilderness in others, and jungles in others.

The need to bring cities under control, to make them safe for the masculine pursuits of profit, politics and power, required also that male control be exerted 'down there', in the deep recesses of the sewers where corruption and infection were rampant and all that was unlawful held sway. The great engineering feats of sewer construction became reassurances of that control, and, although as Trollope observed, 'out of sight was out of mind', it proved less easy a task to banish nature, and the natural, once and for all.

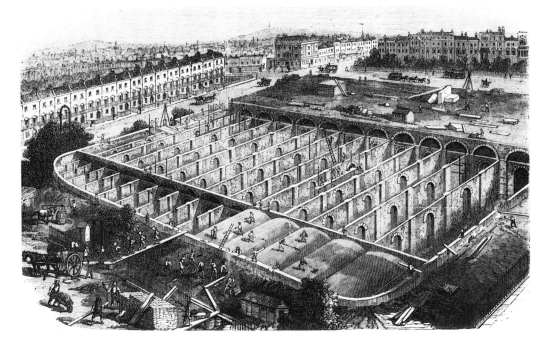

A wood engraving from the *Illustrated London News* of 22 November 1856 showing the reconstruction of the storage reservoir at Claremont Square, part of the New River Waterworks.

191

Chapter eight

INFORMATION

■ *'People are frightened by the thought of too much information, which just shows we're not in the Information Age yet ... Are you frightened by the thought of getting too much money? Too much happiness?'*

ARNO PENZIAS, *Director of Research at AT&T Labs*[1]

Computers are an important accessory in the busy offices of London City dealers.

[1] Quoted in James Gleick, 'The Telephone Transformed – Into Almost Everything', *The New York Times Magazine* (16 May 1993), p. 29.

VIDEOWAY, 'THE FIRST commercially successful interactive television system', had been operating for four years in Montreal when surveys revealed what use customers were making of it. They used the system for 8.5 hours per week, of which four hours were spent playing video games, three hours on watching interactive programmes like the game show *Jeopardy*, and 1.5 hours were devoted to 'data services', the most popular of which are weather reports, horoscopes and lotteries. One customer welcomed the chance to have some say in the programmes: 'You might be seeing the interactive news and think: "I'm tired of the war in Bosnia. Let's see a different story".'[2]

Welcome to the Information Age! According to its enthusiastic advocates, we now (or soon will) live in a world blessed by an information infrastructure of computers, tied to each other and a host of telecommunication peripherals such as FAX machines, television sets, and telephones by 'super-highway' networks. This infrastructure will 'enrich our lives by relieving us of mundane tasks, by improving the ways we live, learn and work and by unlocking new personal and social freedoms'. The result will be 'that computers and networks will democratize human communication,' permitting the 'formation of electronic tribes that can span physical distance.'[3] They will also bring vast profits to some, 'cybersex' to others, and make 'smart' everything from battlefields to automobiles, and buildings to people.

The ranks of the information evangelists consist largely of entrepreneurs who see great profit in it for themselves, of technical specialists who feel they will be able to present their own expertise as being more valuable than that of others, people who believe their work and lives will be made easier, and technology enthusiasts thrilled by the dramatic possibilities of use of the elaborating system.

But like all new technologies, those associated with the Information Age are neither as benevolent as their supporters promise, nor are they likely to be as blocked as those who might fear the consequences. They are, in the end, only social relations materialized.

This 'Information Age' is said to have begun in the 1950s when IBM first sold mainframe computers to business corporations. Developed during the Second

[2] (Cleveland) *Plain Dealer*, 23 June 1993. Taken from the *New York Times*.

[3] Michael L. Dertouzos, 'Communications, Computers and Networks', *Technology Review*, 265 (September, 1991), 62, 69.

World War for military purposes, the many uses to which computers are now put were not foreseen by the scientists and engineers who designed them. Over the decades computers became not only smaller, cheaper and more powerful, but also easier to operate for people who had no particular technical ability. By 1993, of the 92 million households in the United States, 25 million had personal computers. This number does not include the countless other millions that could be found in automobiles, microwave ovens, telephone answering machines, coffee-makers, and a host of other consumer durables.

While the personal computer (PC) was spreading to private homes, computers were also being introduced into the workplace. This was their first non-governmental use, but the earliest mainframe installations tended to be used to regulate production in such sites as electric power stations, petroleum refineries, and factory assembly lines, in service industries such as banking and insurance where they were used for data processing, and at universities where they facilitated scientific research. Over the past decade, however, in certain business firms, the idea is popular that most, if not all, employees should have a computer on their desk. During the 1980s alone, American business spent an astonishing $1 trillion on information technology. The contribution this spending has made to corporate prosperity has been variously calculated, but some studies find the return on investment to be fifty-four per cent for manufacturing and sixty-four per cent for business as a whole. It is estimated, for example, that, in the early 1990s, in retail banking, American workers were thirty-two per cent more productive than German and thirty-six per cent more than British workers. The difference was attributed entirely to the use of information technology.[4]

One important aspect of the way that technology has been used is captured in the term 're-engineering'. This term refers not so much to the tools of production as to the way they are organized. Frederick Winslow Taylor's system of 'Scientific Management' which reformed the knowledge of how to make things, swept the industrialized nations early in the twentieth century. In close conjunction with the newly-established industrial research laboratories, the efficiency engineers tended to strip shop-floor and office workers of creative responsibility for their work and to introduce a new level of managers whose job it was to plan and innovate. Now research laboratories came up with the new products and techniques,

[4] *Business Week*, No. 3323 (14 June 1993), 58 and *New York Times*, 27 June 1993.

You are looking inside the world's most remarkable business machine . . . the IBM Electronic Calculator. It solves accounting and research problems faster than any other commercial calculator in general use.

GETTING YOUR ANSWERS

. . . at electronic speed!

IBM's vast engineering know-how is helping American business, industry and the Armed Forces get the answers . . . fast. Through its leadership in applying electronic principles to calculators and other types of punched card business machines, IBM has given greater speed, accuracy and economy to the nation's vital processes of calculating and accounting.

Already thousands of IBM Electronic Business Machines are in everyday use. We are continuing to manufacture them in quantity . . . as fast as quality production will permit.

INTERNATIONAL BUSINESS MACHINES
590 MADISON AVENUE · NEW YORK 22, N. Y.

and management planned the introduction of these innovations into the process of mass production.

The re-engineering that took place during the 1980s and 90s called all this into question. As one commentator noted grimly, 'people who don't add value are going to be in trouble'.[5] A large number of those who 'don't add value' turned out to be middle managers who had been hired to pass information up and down the chain of command, but now could be replaced by a computer. Even more radically, as in the 'Lean Production' model pioneered by Toyota in Japan, information could be given directly to workers who were then expected to show both creativity and initiative. In 1993 one executive of General Electric was quoted as saying that 'all of the good ideas – all of them – come from the hourly workers'.[6] The statement was perhaps an exaggeration, but revealed an old and long-neglected truth: that the people who know how to do things are those who know how to do them better. Re-engineering, at its most radical, was supposed to call into question all the inherited business forms and traditions, from the way in which firms are organized to the way that their products are made and even sold. The re-engineered firm would be built, from the ground up, around its information infrastructure.

Some workers are resisting the changes in the workplace which they perceive as undermining their authority. When doctors at the University of Virginia Hospital were asked to file their drug orders and instructions for treatment by computer, they staged a protest. It has long been known that the proliferation of medical specialists and tests has tended to divide and separate the information needed to make the best possible diagnosis, but also that those same disparate data could be reintegrated by computer. Doctors have resisted this innovation too, reportedly because it might allow nurses to exercise more independent judgement at the bedside.

While the computer is perhaps the key technology of the information infrastructure, it is certainly not the only nor the most common one. The entire field of telecommunications technology is taken to be an integral part of the system. Telephones, still monopolized by the state in many countries, have changed radically during the past decade. Digital dialling is an important part of the change, but so are mobile phones (including those installed in automobiles), those

Left: a 1950s advertisement for an IBM electronic calculator.
Right: a modern digital dialling telephone.

[5] Quoted in *Business Week*, No. 3323 (14 June 1993), 58.
[6] *Ibid.*, 59.

which have a memory for a menu of numbers and dial them at the press of a button, and others which put one call 'on hold' while another is answered. Telephones can now display the number of the incoming caller. Others, not yet successfully marketed, allow callers to see each other as they talk. The telephone also has the obvious advantage of being widely available and simple to use.

Tied to the computer, the telephone can also be used for 'voice mail'. In this system, a caller is automatically given a recorded 'menu' of choices, to be made by pressing one or another of the numbered buttons on the phone. Although users often find the system confusing and unsatisfactory, it has spread rapidly throughout the business world. One bank in a large American city handles seventy per cent of its customer calls by voice mail.[7] One problem that has surfaced concerns the '#' button on telephone receivers. The tone assigned to this symbol is often used to instruct the computer to transfer or disconnect calls. As it turns out, some people, most of whom are women, have voices that are close enough to the '#' tone to trigger a computer response.[8] Men with high voices and some regional accents have the same effect. This is, no doubt, a problem that can be solved by a 'technological fix', but it serves to remind us how easily class and gender biases can be, even unwittingly, encoded into our technology.

The facsimile (FAX) machine is, in a way, only a special kind of telephone. It, too, has become widely used over the past few years, and sometimes with unforeseen results. It is said, for example, that collective action or a strike by British postal workers now has progressively less impact because so much business correspondence travels by FAX today. A signal feature of the Chinese pro-democracy movement, and the aftermath of the Tiananmen Square massacre, was the flurry of faxes that carried the news to the West and sent messages of support back to China from students studying abroad.

After the telephone, television is perhaps the most widespread of telecommunications technologies. Broadcast experimentally in the 1920s, commercial telecasting began on the eve of the

Above left: using a videophone. **L**eft: a fax machine. Right: testing a telephone for sound quality in British Telecom's anechoic chamber which is totally echo-free.

[7] *Ibid.*, 60.
[8] *USA Today*, 14 May 1992.

DAYLIGHT TELEVISION

Recommended by eye specialists!

G-E Price Leader!
Big screen, nearly as wide as the cabinet itself! 10" conventional tube. Long range. Simplified tuning. Compact, rich rosewood plastic cabinet, only 11½" wide. Model 805.

Hᴇʀᴇ's the television you view in a *fully lighted room*...recommended by leading eye specialists and the medical press. It's G-E Daylight Television—brighter than ordinary television by at least 80% under the same conditions. See how wonderfully different your eyes feel as you watch this television, not in darkness but with the lights on! Join the thousands upon thousands who are finding that this great new General Electric advance is easier on the eyes! Model 806, above. 10" tube. Long range—gets distant stations in fringe areas.

Daylight bright, daylight clear, daylight sharp pictures. Compact, genuine mahogany veneered cabinet. Only 13½ inches wide—fits anywhere. Be sure to see model 806.

General Electric Company, Electronics Park, Syracuse, New York

New G-E Clock Radio
America's bedtime favorite. Soothes you to sleep with music, then turns itself off! Wakes you to music, too. G-E electric clock. Tells time in dark. Model 65 in ivory plastic. **$36.95***
(In rosewood plastic, Model 64—**$34.95***)

*Prices slightly higher West and South—subject to change without notice.

You can put your confidence in —

GENERAL ELECTRIC

Second World War and became a virtually indispensable household item in the 1950s. Today, television peripherals like remote-control units, cable hookups and VRC videotape players and recorders have already extended the way in which TVs are used. 'Shopping' channels are now available which allow one to view merchandise and then order it by telephone. Payment is made by credit card.

One proponent for the Information Age has admitted candidly that 'the glorious possibilities ... stem more from opportunism than they do from pressing human needs'.[9] The opportunity better to integrate computer and tele-communications components and functions certainly appears irresistible. Suppose that one's home computer, telephone, and television were all integrated so that one could view merchandise, order a product, have it recorded, and debited from one's bank account, all at one key stroke? More radically, it has been suggested that someone wishing to buy a new car, for example, might view a variety of features on screen at home, and then select those options that suited best. This process would lead to a custom-built vehicle. The choices, made on the home computer, would be fed directly and instantly into the manufacturer's computer, where the parts and subassemblies would be automatically ordered and scheduled. The result would be something that already appears in Japanese factories, 'the mass production of individualized products.'[10]

Portable lap-top computers now on the market contain not only built-in printers but FAX machines as well. Com-puter monitors of TV-quality picture res-olution (accuracy) allow actual moving pictures, not just graphics, to be displayed, and CD-ROMs (Compact Disc Read Only Memory) containing entire sets of ency-clopaedia, for example, can be called to the screen to show text, maps, photo-graphs, and so forth.

One key to integrating these various technologies, and therefore functions, is through the adoption of standardized specifications and protocols. Because the

Left: General Electric's advertisement for their Daylight Television set.

[9] Dertouzos, 64.
[10] Ibid., 68.

Lap-top computers have become one of the most useful forms of portable technology.

United States in the 1940s adopted a technically inferior television standard, videos made by the superior British system cannot be played in America without first being converted. Standardizing too soon can be as dangerous as doing so too late. The situation with computers, even at this late date, is little short of chaotic: different operating systems, different density floppy discs, printers that will not operate automatically with certain computers, different word-processing softwares, and incomprehensible instruction manuals.

During the 1980s HDTV (High Definition Television) was assumed to be the next step in TV development, but there was little agreement on which system to pursue. When in 1986 the United States suggested that Japan's system be made standard, Europe's electronics industry spent $750 million to develop its own, *European* system, based on European technology and presumably safe from Japanese and American competition. It proved to be a misguided effort, but one that underscored the importance of standardizing systems in general.[11] In 1993 a consortium in the United States finally reached a technical consensus on the fact that HDTV should be digital, guaranteeing not only a very high quality of both sound and pictures, but also making it compatible with other, computer-based technologies. The consortium includes such organizations as American Telephone & Telegraph, the Massachusetts Institute of Technology, Zenith Electronics, Thomson Consumer Electronics of France, and Philips Electronics of the Netherlands – and its decision seems likely to compel worldwide acceptance.[12]

Today one can choose to send a message through the post, by telephone, by E-mail using one's computer, or by FAX. All but the first rely on telephone lines to carry messages, supplemented, for long distances, by satellite technology. These networks which tie together computers, telephones, and other devices, are the roadways over which information travels. As with automobiles, information traffic can move quickly along motorways but can encounter congestion if it is switched off onto secondary roads. The nearer one gets to one's destination, the slower one must travel because of narrow streets, stop signs, and so forth. For telephones, the basic road material is copper wire, which is now scarcely adequate for the increased demands of computer traffic. Solving the network problem is a critical need of the Information Age.

More than a decade ago France committed itself to building a data highway,

[11] *Science*, 260 (18 June 1993), 1737.
[12] *San Francisco Chronicle*, 25 May 1993.

Minitel, at an estimated cost of $10 000 per customer. Japan is planning to put one in place, and in the United States there is debate not whether such a highway ought to be built, but who would use it, who should build it, and what technology should be used. A US government report in 1990 warned that, 'if government wants to promote the effective use of new communication technologies to improve the economy and enrich people's lives, it must find ways to deal with issues such as network modernization, standards and the standards-setting process, network security and survivability, education and training, and international trade'.

An even more vexing problem is what might be deemed communication equity. Still operating under the 1934 Communication Act, the government has a mandate to guarantee 'universal service'. The Office of Technology Assessment has warned that 'the gap between those who can access communication services and use information strategically and those who cannot is likely to increase'. The latter group includes 'the poor, the educationally disadvantaged, the geographically and technologically isolated, and the small and medium-sized business'.[13] No technology, nor any national infrastructure, will automatically reflect or promote democratic values. The truism that the rich tend to get richer is equally applicable to the benefits of communication.

Probably the best known information network now operating worldwide is Internet; it had 2000 users in 1981 and has 15 million today. New users are currently being hooked up at the rate of a million a month. Begun in 1969 as a means of exchanging information for American scientists and engineers working on defence research projects, it was demonstrated to the public in 1972. In 1980 a protocol was developed which allowed different networks to be linked. Three years later the defence users were peeled off and given their own network. Internet was dedicated to civilian use and made freely available, worldwide.

[13] 'Critical Connections: Communication for the Future', *OTA Report Brief* (January, 1990).

Although the network was designed by and for scientists, by 1993 only a third of the users were in that category.[14] Although these account for forty-eight per cent of the use, ten per cent is used by the defence services, six per cent by educators other than scientists, seven per cent by governments, and twenty-nine per cent by commercial interests.[15]

The heady potential of more than 15 million customers has created a scramble among those who hate to see the government making a network available free, when users might be charged for the service. In 1990 a consortium of IBM, the MCI Communications Corporation, and a group of Michigan universities began discussions with the government over the possible establishment of a non-profit corporation to operate a new, national network. Then in the spring of 1993 Tele-Communications, Inc., America's largest cable television company, announced plans to lay a $2 billion fibre-optic cable across the nation, tying together 400 communities.

The plan is to replace the older technology of coaxial cables with the fibre-optic cable on the main trunk lines, like large, cross-country superhighways. This method uses pulses of light to carry information and greatly increases the amount of information that can be moved, virtually instantaneously. Fibre-optic cables will be laid to neighbourhoods; from there data will be carried by local coaxial cables, which are being upgraded by a process called digital compression. This allows the cable to carry more information – the equivalent of an increase from the present fifty to a hoped-for 850 TV channels.[16] The $2 billion would bring service to only 400 communities, however. Estimates for a fibre-optic network that would serve the whole country range up to $300 billion. Already the state of Iowa has begun its own network, planned to reach each of the state's ninety-nine counties, three universities, fifteen community colleges, eleven private colleges, eight public television stations, and all major state government offices. All 2600 miles of fibre-optic cable will be laid by the end of 1993. Plans then call for an extension to all 351 high schools and more than 500 public libraries, and, perhaps, to all hospitals as well.[17]

The alternative would be simply to upgrade the nation's telephone system, which already reaches more homes even than television cables. The digital compression carried out by Tele-Communications is being used by telephone companies as well, and service is continually being expanded. The last three area codes

[14] 'The Rocky Road to a Data Highway', *Science*, 260 (21 May 1993), 1064.
[15] *San Francisco Chronicle*, 1 June 1993.
[16] *New York Times*, 12 April 1993.
[17] *New York Times*, 5 March 1993.

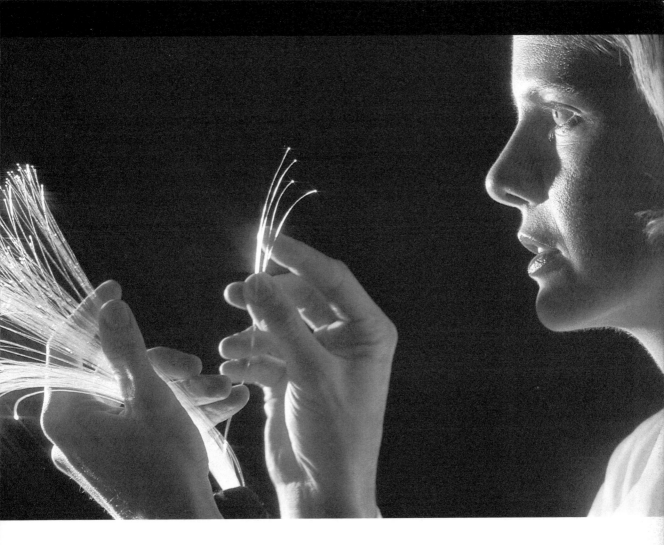

■ *We're talking about hundreds of billions of dollars.*

ARTHUR BUSHKIN, *Corporate Executive*[18]

Above: fibre-optic filaments. Each one is less than 1 mm in diameter and is made from a special glass which is flexible and has a high refractive index.

[18] Quoted in *Newsweek*, 121 (31 May 1993), 40.

available in North America have recently been used up, and more trans-Atlantic circuits have been opened in the last three years than in any previous period.[19] The race is on to see who will capture *the* information network, and both cable television and telephone companies are determined to win.

With advanced computers and telecommunications devices tied into networks by fibre-optic superhighways transmitting data at speed of a billion bits (gigabits) per second, it is tempting to think that our lives must surely be altered in dramatic and, presumably, positive ways. Already some people are 'computing' to work, turning homes and automobiles into offices which, through FAX and E-mail, are in constant touch with the corporate headquarters. In rural New England, a nineteenth-century gristmill has been converted to offices where stock brokers communicate with Wall Street in New York by computer – the electricity for which is produced by turbines and generators utilizing the mill's waterpower. At the other end of the work ladder, thousands of women work on data processing on computers at home, where they can be with their children. But they have no benefits, no unions, and are paid by piece rate.

If homes are turning into offices, the traditional offices themselves are beginning to disappear. One consulting firm in California has taken offices away from an experimental group of account managers and given them computers at home instead. Rather than spend time at the office, or commuting to and from it, the managers go directly from home to see clients, updating and downloading files

[19] James Gleick, 'The Telephone Transformed – Into Almost Everything', *The New York Times Magazine*, 16 May 1993.

electronically. If they need to call at the headquarters, they book a vacant office in advance: just-in-time offices for an age of lean production. Hotels, which have always been the loci of new technologies, now have business centres as well as exercise areas.

Those who must still commute to work may someday use the smart car and the smart highway. These date at least to the 1950s. Systems of traffic lights that sense the flow of vehicles and change lights accordingly are now so common as to be unnoticed. But in the future people may be able to take advantage of IVHS (Intelligent Vehicle or Highway Systems), made up of five components: 1) Advanced Traffic Management Systems (ATMS), 2) Advanced Traveller Information Systems (ATIS), 3) Advanced Public Transit Systems (APTS), 4) Commercial Vehicle Operations (CVO) and 5) Automatic Vehicle Control Systems (AVCS). In the world of acronyms and technical jargon, 'Advanced' usually denotes a product that doesn't yet work, or at least not completely. However, some of these components were put to experimental use in Orlando, Florida in the spring of 1992. A hundred Oldsmobile Toronados have been equipped with computer-driven maps, automatic location systems, audio systems, and routing software.

The United States government put $3 million into IVHS in 1990, $20 million in 1991, and $234 million for 1992, including an Intermodal Surface Transportation and Efficiency programme. Enthusiasts predict that a total of $220 billion will be invested during the next twenty years. Similar programmes such as PROMETHEUS and DRIVE are underway in Europe. Japan has RACS and AMTICS.[20]

Perhaps the most sensational change is what one headline termed the promise of 'Sex Without Human Complications'. Readers of Aldous Huxley's novel *Brave New World* have always been titillated by his description of 'feelies', films that viewers not only saw and heard, but also *felt*. In an age not only of information but also of AIDS, the prospect of 'cybersex' has a certain attraction, at least for some. A few years ago, the French information network spawned a widespread (and expensive) sex bulletin board where users, protected by the armour of hardware and the veil of passwords, could communicate in terms that would be forbidden to polite society. In the United States a less high-tech industry, based on the telephone and credit cards, allows customers of certain 900 area code numbers to exchange obscenities with an entire menu of 'types'. Sexually improper

[20] Richard P. Braun, 'Smart highways, smart cars, smarter people', *APWA Reporter*, 59 (June, 1992), 2.

videos are widely available to anyone with a TV and VCR. In San Francisco, a new journal, *Future Sex*, has been a pioneer in the field of 'cyberporn'.

Cybersex is made possible through the technology of 'virtual reality'. A person can become a 'virtual' participant in three-dimensional reality in a video game. To do this players wear a helmet with a special visor, and use electronic manual controls. There are already popular games that involve tracking down, or raping women, for example. Or one can rescue a woman threatened by rape. The promise of virtual reality is that one can actually take part in the activities, not just help control them. That 'cybersex' might encourage antisocial habits, or lead to a new degree of solitary satisfaction, is denied by the editor of *Future Sex*. 'The sparkling wizardry of erototronics', she has asserted, 'will quickly seem as ho-hum as boiling water in the microwave if it's seen as the apex, rather than the accessory.'[21]

This is a scenario for the future. Meanwhile, as one observer says, 'Internet has proven a remarkably effective means of distributing pornography, both text and graphic images.'[22] The ultimate consequence of women being regarded as objects in our society has been their identification with technology. The appalling misogynist joke, that a wife is an appliance which, when screwed in the bed, does all the housework, is hardly a product of the Information Age, but it does suggest that patterns of subjugation are more difficult to change than technologies.

The nation which seems to be leading the rest of the world into this brave new Information Age is Japan. Nearly a quarter of a century ago it was reported that Expo '70 in Japan was 'a landscape of glittering laser beams, clicking computers and clanking robots.'[23] Members of the press grumbled that much of the spectacle represented smoke and mirrors, not high-tech. Two decades later the country had a solid reputation for quality products, manufacturing wizardry, and a systematic plan for the development and application of information technology. The awkward word 'informatization' has been coined to describe the goal, and the Ministry of International Trade and Industry (MITI) has declared it one of the most important bases for continued economic growth and prosperity in Japan.

Informatization represents the penetration of information technologies into as many aspects and nooks and crannies of life as possible. A report by the Japan Information Processing Development Center in 1991, for example, examines the

Virtual reality can be used to create almost any situation. In this case 'virtual sex'.

[21] Quoted in (Cleveland) *Plain Dealer*, 19 November 1992.
[22] Adam Begley, 'Electrotalk Therapy: Sex, Politics, and Paranoia on the Net', *Lingua Franca*, 3 (January/February, 1993), 50.
[23] *New York Times*, 22 March 1970.

'The Spread of Informatization – To Industry and to Individuals.'[24] Under 'Informatization of Daily Life and Society and the Individual', the report notes the intrusion of television, FAX machines, multifunctional telephones, and computers into the Japanese home. Devices using 'fuzzy processing', or the technology that can, for example analyse a laundry load of mixed white and coloured clothing, and then select the optimal water temperature and amount of soap, are gaining in popularity. Because of increased 'social activities' of women, they can order goods to be delivered at home at a specified time.

Computers had been installed in only forty-six per cent of state schools in Japan by 1991, but a plan, begun the previous year, was meant to place computers in all schools within five years. MITI also coined the term 'Mellow Society' to indicate the advantages of the information age to older people, an important goal in a society that expects to be the 'most aged society in the very near future'.

Equipment was also being redesigned to allow for better access by the physically handicapped. This same desire to make each individual in society familiar with, and have access to, information technologies, extends to the workplace.

Computers can be used to improve children's reading skills with special packages.

[24] Information on this subject taken from JIPDEC, *Informatization White Paper* (Tokyo: JIPDEC, 1991).

The report showed that types of businesses varied widely in their use of information technologies, but the ideal was stated in terms of 'intelligent buildings', which, as a matter of course, would provide a computer for each worker. There was a widespread belief that, in a nation without a great abundance of natural resources and a worsening labour shortage, 'information' was the most readily available 'value' to add to goods and services. Because 'daily livers', as those employees who perform 'intelligent' office work were called, spent much more time at work than at home, 'intelligent' buildings were also being made 'comfortable'. Special furniture, disco dancing contests, air conditioning and other examples of comfort quoted were hardly new or high-tech, but they represented one extreme of trying to reform an increasingly alienating workplace.

At the other extreme was the belief, rapidly becoming commonplace, that work needn't be always done 'at work', but might be performed at home, or in regional offices deliberately located away from Tokyo, sometimes even in resort areas. MITI announced a 'New Media Community' plan to try to get corporations to move away from the metropolis. The small city of Bibai, in Hokkaido province, provided a striking example of creative response. Located only a forty-minute train ride from the provincial city of Sapporo, Bibai boasted land prices as low as a hundredth of those in Tokyo. The city was installing satellite facilities which would allow for the continuous communication of vast amounts of data: already in 1991 several large software firms had moved their operations there. One of these gave each of its employees a lap-top computer and encouraged them to work at home. With work-stations for every employee, and the equipping of every home with fibre optics by 2015, it is planned that all of Japan will become 'informationized'.

The spectre, as also the reality, of Japanese success with information technologies has not gone unchallenged in the West. Britain's Alvey program, a five-year research effort in reply to Japan's 'fifth-generation' computer programme, sought to bring computer companies, university researchers, and electronics manufacturers into a consortium that would 'develop the generic technologies needed to strengthen Britain's fragmented information-technology industry'. After spending £200 million, however, the industry was worse off than before. On the one hand, companies proved unwilling to share even 'pre-competitive' research with their rivals. At the same time, devastating economic conditions took their toll: by the end of the project, four of the five participating semiconductor makers were out of business or had been absorbed by some other firm.

The former director of the project commented in 1991 that 'the UK was foolish enough to think that prosperity can be based simply on research – a belief which stems from the Second World War when radar was wired together by scientists in the evenings.'[25] A similar lesson might be drawn from the European Community's largest research programme, Esprit. The oldest of the many international industrial research projects, and aimed specifically at information technologies, it was launched in 1984. In its latest phase, covering 1990–94, it is spending $1.8 billion on the same sort of pre-competitive research attempted by Alvey.

Esprit has served as a model for other programmes such as RACE (for communications technology), BRITE/EURAM (materials and manufacturing technologies), and TELEMATICS (data-exchange techniques). One of Esprit's more successful efforts was to help Britain's Inmos corporation to come up with a parallel processing chip called a 'transputer'. Despite some successes, it has been decided that 'the programme's strategy needs a rethink to couple research more closely to the marketplace'.[26] As late as 1978, Europe's balance of trade in information and communications technology was about even, but by 1991 it had developed a $40 billion deficit.

Despite archaic innovation strategies and a long and severe recession in the West, it is Japan's success that is most often singled out to explain western failure. In 1989 Japan replaced Russia as the nation Americans feared most, and the openly racist remarks about 'ants' and 'little yellow men' by the then French Prime Minister, Edith Cresson, show that this fear is a Western, not simply American phenomenon. In part, it is a reaction to memories of aggression and atrocities during the Second World War, but such memories tend to be selective and other factors are at work here.

David Morley and Kevin Robins, in a paper on 'Techno-Orientalism', claim that 'the association of technology and Japaneseness now serves to reinforce the image of a culture that is cold, impersonal and machine-like, an authoritarian culture lacking emotional connection to the rest of the world. The *otaku* generation – kids "lost to everyday life" by their immersion in computer

[25] Quoted in *Science*, 252 (31 May 1991), 1248.
[26] *Science* 260 (June 18, 1993), 1736.

WELCOME TO WARP ZONE!

4 3 2

reality – provides a strong symbol of this.'[27] Just as the baton of technological vanguardism was passed from Great Britain to the United States in the nineteenth century, it seems now to have crossed the Pacific Ocean to Japan. And just as that first passage coincided with the rise of the modern, so the second has seemed to coincide with the rise of the post-modern.

At the heart of the concept of *orientalism* is the West's claim to universality, to being the subject in relation to which objects are defined. We are modern, they are not. We are normal, they are not. We can be assumed, they must be explained. They are, in short, not us. For example, Australians have until recently thought of China and Japan as the 'Far East'. Now they have realized that, by any reasonable reading of the map, those countries are actually the 'Near North'. One

Above: wearing a special power glove this child can play a virtual reality video game.

[27] David Morley and Kevin Robins, 'Techno-Orientalism: Futures, Foreigners and Phobias', *New Formations*.

particular expression of this distorted view can be particularized by gender. Men are the subject, women the object. It is women who are different; in a way they are not even 'modern' (that is they are natural and emotional), and must be explained. To the extent then that the West accepts modernity as a signal characteristic of its self-definition, and technology (almost always seen as masculine in our society) is the most significant engine and marker of modernity, to lose its vanguard position in matters technological is to lose subjectivity, to be marginalized, and to feel emasculated. The West invented modernity and used it to explain and justify its claim to universality. Now history, it seems, has moved beyond modernity to post-modernity, and this new world is defined and dominated by Japan, an 'Oriental' nation which can no longer be measured by western and modern standards.

The term 'post-modern' does nothing to reveal its own nature. Clearly it is meant to come after modern, but even if we had a clear notion of what 'modern' meant, it gives no hint of what comes next. It is a term borrowed from art history, like Renaissance, in which context it refers to buildings at the same time eclectic and playful, borrowing freely from historical styles and depending upon that borrowing for a style of its own. In some ways, that could stand also as a definition of the Information Age – all medium with no particular message of its own. When the critic Jean Baudrillard argues that, 'in the future, power will belong to those peoples with no origins and no authenticity', he was defining a post-modern people, fully integrated with their machines, living 'virtual' lives sustained by gigabits of 'information'. The contemporary conflation of news and entertainment, fact and fiction, 'smart' wars and video games, sex and 'erototronics', make it 'virtually' impossible to draw a clear and comfortable distinction between the real and unreality or, perhaps, between 'authentic' people and 'replicants', to borrow a category from the film *Bladerunner*.

The Enlightenment project has always drawn upon its own base of universality to define a steadily improving world, made ever more modern through the creative destruction of a steadily changing technology. From the first *philosophe* to the latest dictator, it is the 'Future' that has been invoked to justify the present. The Future has been defined largely in terms of technology and the literature of Tomorrow abounds with the concepts detailing the sublimity of technology. Over

The use of a headset with video screens allows the cyclist to travel through a computer-generated landscape. If she achieves certain speeds the bicycle can appear to take off and fly!

the past century and a half novels about utopias, science fiction, world's fairs, corporate advertising and an entire genre of magazines have touted the wonders of the City of Tomorrow, the Home of the Future, a World Without Work, the Defeat of Nature, Magic Bullets, and perhaps even Victory over Death.

Drawing heavily upon both the sacred promise of Millenialism and the profane Enlightenment project, the United States has, from its many beginnings, thought of itself as representing the future of humankind in distinction to an Old World anchored in the past. It is not surprising, therefore, that Americans took the joyous prediction of technology most to heart and now feel most sensibly the threat of Japanese supremacy. The historian Joseph J. Corn has concluded that, despite the fact that such optimistic predictions usually have been 'erroneous, exaggerated, or wildly utopian', most Americans, save for a sceptical minority, have embraced them as true visions of the future.[28]

Their poor record in accuracy Corn attributes to three factors. First, there has been a tendency to assume that important new technologies will sweep the field, driving competing technologies completely off the market and out of use. In reality, even so radical a new technology as nuclear power merely joins with hydro-electric and fossil-fuel fired plants to present an ensemble of sources for generating electricity. If this first misunderstanding overestimates the revolutionary nature of change, the second mistake – what Corn calls the 'fallacy of social continuity' – underestimates change. It assumes that radical new machines will easily slip into well-understood social niches. The inventors of the computer, for example, assumed that only a few would be needed by scientists and large corporations because it would be used only to solve very large, very important mathematical problems. They did not envisage microchips, let alone their use by Nintendo. Finally, the fallacy of the technological fix led to the assumption that new devices would solve old problems, not raise new ones. Although Victor Frankenstein initially agreed to assemble a female companion to placate the destructive monster he had already created, he later realized that he might also thereby be doubling his trouble. In a rare moment of insight and prudence, he destroyed the female counterpart before he had finished making her.

Corn also calls attention to the fact that, however wildly inaccurate predictions of the technological future might prove to be, they have been taken as credible,

Intel's Touchstone Delta system.

[28] 'Epilogue', *Imagining Tomorrow: History, Technology, and the American Future*, ed. Joseph J. Corn (Cambridge: MIT Press, 1986), pp. 219–229.

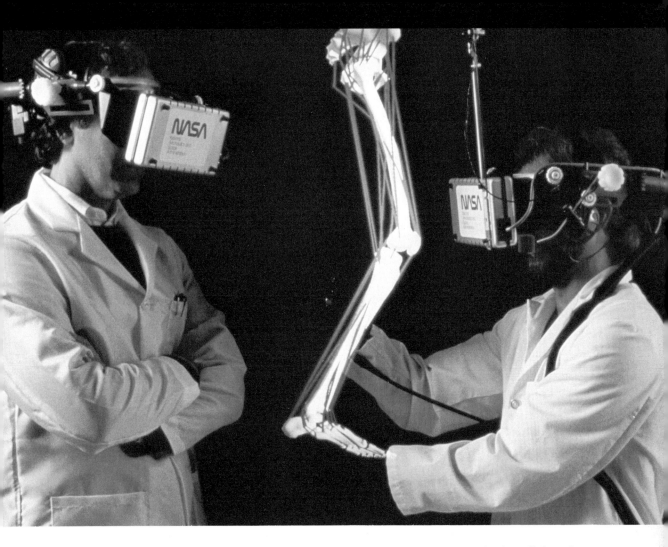

and even desirable by so many people gives them a force as historical realities. A quarter-century ago, James Carey and John Quirk in relating what they called 'The Mythos of the Electronic Revolution' to the celebration of previous 'Ages' – those of Steam, Science, Electricity, and Nuclear Power come readily to mind – warned against the political uses of the technological sublime. The concept of the sublime is borrowed from aesthetics. It suggests not only the awakening of uplifting emotion but of a force so grand that the only proper human response is awe and excitement; certainly not resistance. The technological sublime is invoked to insure acquiescence in the project proposed, and to prevent, or at least marginalize, political opposition.

Above: two doctors use virtual reality to learn about the human leg. They both wear 3-D video displays to view graphical images and gloves with woven optical fibre sensors.

The political efficacy of invoking a 'New Age' lies in the fallacies identified by Corn: the new technology will be totalizing in that all previous forms, and the power and interests that grew from them, are swept away and all social, economic and political relationships must be renegotiated; at the same time only those things can change which are ear-marked for change; and finally, that only a marginalized few will doubt that the emperor is wearing wonderful new clothes. Despite the fact that every previous 'Age' has proved to be something of an artificial construct, the Information Age is now presented as something real and new to the world, and at the same time something inevitable and progressive.

In evaluating this or any other technological 'Age', it is important not only to avoid the pitfalls of technological romanticism but equally to see and think clearly about what tools are, and from whence they come. As the material manifestations of social relations, tools are concrete commitments to certain ways of doing things, and therefore certain ways of dividing power. It is a mistake to think that, like black and white marbles, the 'good' and 'bad' effects of technology can be sorted out and dealt with. In fact, one person's white marbles are another's black: labour saved is jobs destroyed, research investments carry opportunity costs, new advances mean obsolete investment, my loss is your gain. Information (like all) technology is a means not an end, and while it is necessary to remember that the choice of means itself always carries consequences, these are not the same as the human purposes that set them in motion.

When the landscape scholar John Brinkerhoff Jackson returned during the Second World War to a Europe he had travelled, studied, and loved as a young man recently graduated from college, he discovered it filled with 'information' he had not previously been aware of. Before he had learned the origins and purposes of ancient monuments and famous buildings, the style and culture of great cities. As a young intelligence officer with the American forces in Europe he 'grew to know it in greater detail'. In part this was simply because 'both sides had superimposed a military landscape on the landscape of devastation', and he now had to read and interpret the symbols of military life and command. Away from headquarters, however, the physical environment itself contained information that had always been there, but could no longer be ignored. 'In peacetime,' he noted, 'weather and topography – to say nothing of the texture of the soil and the density of the foliage – were never looked upon as of much consequence', and was therefore information which could be ignored.[29] Now the phase of the moon, the crack of a twig, the smell of another human being, could spell death. As killers and looters, the soldiers at the front were modern hunter-gatherers, and for them information was just as vital as in later years it might be to any ambitious corporate executive or government bureaucrat. Jackson's experience reminds us that while we do indeed live in an Information Age, people always have.

Nor are we the first generation to elevate 'information' to a separate and higher meaning. 'Facts alone are wanted in life', says Mr Gradgrind in Charles Dickens' *Hard Times*. 'Plant nothing else, and root out everything else. You can only form the minds of reasoning animals upon Facts; nothing else will ever be of any service to them.'[30] The Utilitarians of the Victorian age not only elevated information (or 'facts') to a powerful political force with their surveys of social conditions, but also hid a liberal political agenda behind a façade of impartiality.

Like other technologies, those organized around the storage, transmission, and analysis of information are hardly neutral. On the most obvious level, and as many even among the enthusiasts have conceded, the resources of money and skills necessary to take advantage of them cannot but widen the gap between those who are already privileged and those who are not. Technology remains a very human tool, used by some against others, and by all to get what benefit is available from that use. Like all past 'Ages', that of Information will prove to have been less totalizing than advertised, and more sweeping than expected. Both, however, can have human meaning only when understood in human terms. As Orientalism has taught us, the Other is always a cultural construction, something we have imagined to better define ourselves. Perhaps this is true of technology as well.

'Personally, I don't think television is all it's cracked up to be'

[29] John Brinkerhoff Jackson, *The Necessity for Ruins, and Other Topics* (Amherst: University of Massachusetts Press, 1980), pp. 11–17.

[30] Quoted in Theodore Roszak, *The Cult of Information: The Folklore of Computers and the True Art of Thinking* (New York: Pantheon Books, 1986), p. 156.

INDEX

Page numbers in **bold** denote illustrations

224